MW01200964

ORGANIC SPIRITUALITY

To
Mary Lou, Joe, Ben, Sam, and Michael Verla
surrogate family and faithful friends.

Contents

Preface

Ten-year-old Sam was on his first camping trip with his dad and the Cub Scouts. He and his father had successfully pitched the tent and he had been left to unroll the sleeping bags while his dad went to consult with the other Scout masters. When his dad returned, he found Sam sprawled out blissfully on top of the sleeping bags in the tent, gazing up at the trees through the open screen with an ecstatic grin on his face. "I *love* this!" he said to his dad with primal glee, thoroughly saturated with delight.

At ten years of age, Sam is in touch with something that many of us forfeit as we grow into adolescence and adulthood. He is reveling in organic awe. He is savoring this moment when everything feels just right. He feels good about himself, in harmony with his world, and he knows something bigger than himself is close at hand. It feels good to be alive. This is a truly spiritual experience.

Many of us confine our spirituality to the narrow parameters of the church building. We tend to equate spirituality with religion and separate it from our capacity for natural awe and wonder. For Sam it is still an integrated experience. He knows a great fullness and satisfaction in this moment of surrender to something "awesome." Not only is he open to it, he has the wisdom to relish it when it comes upon him as

a surprise gift of God, even if he may not apply God's name
to it yet.

This book is about the recovery of our lost appreciation
for the organic elements in our spiritual life. It is meant to
help us identify and consciously foster contemplative dispositions and actions that enhance our spiritual vitality in
everyday life. In addition to acknowledging the contributions of religious tradition to the spiritual life and the factors
that both formatively and deformatively coalesced to shape
the vocational directions of our lives, this book raises our
awareness of the need to recover in our spiritual story "organic" elements of which we may no longer be aware. These
are not lost, but merely need to be articulated as *our story*,
either in writing or in speaking, and reflected upon for new
meaning and vitality to emerge.

The contribution that reflection on the organic influences can offer us is a revitalization of our spiritual life. Our
spiritual life is the "livelihood" from which we make meaning and connect with ourselves, the larger world, and our
God. A recovery of the forgotten organic influences that
moved us in our depths in earlier periods of our lives can
stimulate us on a visceral level now and become formative
for us as adults.

I do not merely want to identify what organic spirituality
is. I also want to assist readers in devising practical ways to
apply organic sensitivity to everyday life. This is a book with
a theory that is supported, therefore, by six organic spiritual
practices on how to deepen our contemplative consciousness. These experiences in daily human life may not be identified as specifically spiritual by any great world religious tradition. However, practiced intentionally, they can enhance
our spiritual lives and lead us into greater maturity in relation to the mystery of God.

It is my hope to assist the reader by providing concrete reflective questions that will stimulate the recovery of organic influences. Having practiced these six spiritual disciplines for many years, I have found a fresh, unstrained attitude toward spirituality emerge within my own life. The "work" of my spiritual life is less a matter of "labor" than of surprise, appreciation, and pleasure. The six spiritual practices presented in this book are not heavy disciplines to be mastered through effort and intensity. Rather, they are six refreshing ways to become aware of the sacred in everyday life as we raise our faces gratefully to God.

It is with a sense of delight that I offer these to you, the reader, so that your spiritual hunger can be satisfied within the reality you face within your own life. There need be no split and no angst in the practice of contemplative consciousness. As a spiritual director once assured me in my struggle to meet God, there is little need to please or attract God. "God is just crazy about you," she said. Knowing that God desires us as much as we desire God makes the spiritual journey a lot easier.

PART ONE
BACKGROUND

A Definition of Spirituality

John was five years old when his adoptive family took him to an uncle's country home for the first time. Scarred by neglect and abuse, he was a quiet child who had retreated into a shell of self-protection. This summer evening, as the car pulled into the driveway, fireflies were erupting across the yard in front of the house. John was transfixed. Getting out of the car, he stood amazed at this wonderful display of light and transience. He stood his ground when the relatives tried to prevail upon him to come inside. This was a spectacle too precious to miss and they would not deprive him of it. Sensing the gift of this moment, the family wisely allowed him to linger for five more minutes alone on the front porch.

He is now in his forties, and he recalls the event as being one of the most significant in his spiritual formation as a contemplative. A religious brother who suffered through many natural disasters on the missions, he now designates that moment as a moment of hope and ecstasy. It sustains him in his ongoing healing process. He finds new meaning and experiences gratitude each time he reflects upon that summer night.

The mystery is all around us, using any means necessary to get our attention. Human wisdom has tried to explain it. Religious traditions have evolved from reflection on it. Entire lives have been dedicated to the pursuit of the holy. All of this finds its origin in the transcendent yearnings that first were felt organically in the soul of a child. To remember these moments of insight and inspiration and allow them their full potential to enliven our spirits can lead to a recovery of soul. Spiritual vitality exists right within the hidden places of our story "for those who have eyes to see." As early as the age of five, John had the "eyes to see."

It would be helpful as we begin our exploration of organic spirituality to first of all define what we understand spirituality to mean. There are many good definitions from which we could choose. The definition I propose for us in this book is as follows:

SPIRITUALITY IS A GROWING INTIMACY WITH GOD EXPERIENCED THROUGH PERSONS, PLACES, EVENTS, AND THINGS IN EVERYDAY LIFE.[1]

Let's take the definition apart to see what is hidden in these words. Spirituality is a "growing intimacy." First of all, when we use the word "growing," we presume a certain dynamism, a newness; we are not talking about something static. This definition of spirituality refers to a relationship with God that was not completed at age twelve when many of us finished our formal religious education. Something is continuing to move interiorly, even though at times we may regress or become restless as we wait. There is an ongoing engagement that is forming us.

The definition refers to intimacy with God. Intimacy is about the "deepest things." It connotes "something of a personal and private nature," according to Webster's dictionary. Webster goes on to say that the word "intimate" is "marked by a very close association, contact, or familiarity."[2] Therefore, spirituality infers that we are willing to enter into a close familiarity with the divine, a familiarity that is accessible not only in the rarified moments of retreat and deliberate religious experience, but also within the everyday moments of our regular life. All other relationships of intimacy, whether with one's self, each other, or the world at large, flow from this primal intimacy with the mystery who created us. All of these other intimacies eventually can lead us back to original intimacy with the divine.

In Christianity, this forming mystery has the name of "God." Other traditions may identify this mystery by other names (e.g., Allah, Yahweh) and may speak about the mystery in a variety of forms; all of them recognize that there is something bigger than ourselves which permeates the cosmos. In our spiritual lives, we attempt to engage with this mystery on a regular basis. The more serious we are about engaging with God, the more we will build habitual practices that enable our intimacy to be fostered.

When it comes to relating to the divine, we are speaking of uncovering an intimacy that is organically as close to us as it was to ten-year-old Sam described in the preface. The mystery of God is always close by, anticipating our willingness to enter into intimacy, aching for our consent and our attentiveness.

With this in mind, where do we turn to see the mystery of God, who seems somewhat hidden from us, but is reaching toward us? Let us return to our definition. Spirituality is a growing intimacy with God experienced through persons, places, events, and things in everyday life. The definition clues us in to look for the presence of God within the persons, places, events, and things that surround us, within the milieu in which we live. God uses all of the seemingly mundane realities around us to teach us about ourselves, our relationships, and our God.

Organic spirituality invites us to return to our own story and identify some of the persons, places, events, and things through which God has revealed God's self. These may have been so embedded within everyday life that they escaped our awareness as were growing up. Now, with adult eyes, we can look back gently and deliberately to discover their spiritual benefit and to recognize their spiritual significance in a deeper way than we could have previously. With a more reflective approach, we can look behind the scenes of our story and uncover a surprisingly large store of organic material that can enrich us now in adulthood.

When I was a child, one of my favorite summer pastimes was to wade in a mountain stream with friends. Inevitably, we would stop to dig out colorful rocks which caught our attention as we slowly stepped through the water. Something would attract us and we would pause, pull out a rock and hold it up to see it in the light. We would also find ourselves drawn to the pocket of sand that had formed around the rock. The water creatures, mud, and pebbles were all fascinating and often held a treasure or two. This is where we look for spiritual treasures... underneath the rocks of everyday life.

Persons: Mentors of Awareness

Let us begin with persons. I like to think of the persons who have influenced my awareness of the mystery of God as "mentors of awareness" of the sacred. By word or by action these people turned my face toward this "bigger than" mystery that I later came to name "God." Their instruction may have been verbal in that they spoke openly about their experience of God and encouraged me to do the same.

There are also those who more silently taught me about this presence that is beyond me. Something in their demeanor and attentiveness to the mystery attracted me and opened me to reverence and awe. I also learned from their wordless display of respect.

During my childhood, my mother was someone with whom I could speak frankly about my fascination with this mystery. I could ask her questions about God and knew that she would speak from both personal experience and religious knowledge. She was the one who taught us our prayers as children. Kneeling beside her each evening, we carefully repeated the words she spoke and then begged her to teach us another prayer. If we had been good that day, she would gladly do so.

My mother was so attentive to this hunger in me for the mystery that when, at the age of fifteen, I indicated a curiosity about scripture, she did some research at the local parish to determine which translation would be most attractive and suitable for an adolescent and then presented me with my first copy of the New Jerusalem Bible, "just because." There was no special event like a birthday to serve as a reason for this gift. It was merely her response to my desire. I could take my questions to her and she would to the best of her ability candidly share her answers to the questions and her reflections on them. She modeled for me the acceptability of speaking of faith and of asking questions with regard to religion, spirituality, and God.

My father, on the other hand, was a quieter mentor. He was a stoic farmer-rancher, whose words were few but whose example was deep. In my childhood, he would commute to the farm from the town in which we lived during the winters. Many a morning in Lent I would see the kitchen light and I would sneak out to find him putting on his boots before going to early Mass. I desperately longed for one-on-one time with him and so, when I appeared at the door and lingered, he knew that sending me back to bed was not a viable option. I am sure now that I was intruding upon "something of a personal and private nature" in his familiarity with the divine, but, nevertheless, he would invite me to go along with him. "Go change out of your pajamas," he would say, and in moments the two of us would be rumbling down the hills in the blue jalopy pickup to get to church.

We would usually arrive early, even before the priest had gotten there, and we would sit on the left side in the back (in contrast to my mother's favorite place on Sunday, four pews from the front on the right). No words were said. No instructions were given on squirming or on prayer. Sitting quietly in that space next to him, what I saw was a reverence and a regard for this "Something Big" that even my strong, silent father bowed to. I saw an approach to the sacred that schooled me in contemplative attentiveness. Dad was an unassuming, unintentional mentor of awareness for me. My contemplative consciousness was born at his side.

As children, we need both of these types of mentors. We need the ones who speak of their interest in the divine and the ones who mystify us by their example. Both draw us in to an experience of the sacred that can ground us and instill in us a hunger for more.

It may be helpful now to put this book down and try to recall some of the hidden "mentors of awareness" in your own life. I would even recommend that you take a few moments with a journal and pen and write down the names of those who, now that you reflect on it through your adult consciousness, turned your face toward the sacred and awakened your curiosity and respect for this bigger mystery. The following questions may trigger your reflection:

> *Who modeled respectful attentiveness to mystery and to the sacred?*
>
> *Who could you speak to about this mystery?*
>
> *Who in quiet ways nurtured a contemplative reverence in you?*
>
> *In looking back as an adult, what meaningful messages did you derive from their example?*

Sacred and Safe Places: Geographies for Our Spirits

In addition to significant persons who turned our faces toward the sacred, there may have been special places that nurtured our awareness of mystery. These places may have been designated by our religious tradition as "sacred" in that they were reserved for the holy. When we entered these places, we were automatically filled with an awareness of presence and a sense of awe. Or they may have been natural places which by their magnitude dropped us into an awareness of immensity, an appreciation of beauty, or instantaneous stillness. Equally important were the domestic places where we felt safe, at home inside, and open to "just being."

I remember during recess taking refuge in the church near the Catholic school I attended. I would slip in the side door and be met by the residual smells of incense and beeswax candles and a lingering sense of prayer. Staying close to the wall, I would tiptoe down the side aisle until I could see the tabernacle and the candle that flickered before it. There it was, that familiar beacon of life and light that my father reverenced so obviously. I connected with that presence for which this place was reserved, and I felt a comfort and an intimacy begin to grow inside me during these little "visits." I felt safe here, special, and still. It was a haven from the noise and competition of my peers and I felt welcomed and received. It was definitely a sacred place where someone special lived.

Outside, immensity spread over me each day on the farm. Raised under the big sky of Montana, I spent my summers embraced by a blanket of light blue each morning, gripped by the blazing brilliance of a noonday sun at midday, and comforted by the cool arms of the evening. This sky seemed eternal. It was a theater of extravagant color and majesty as the sun sank slowly each night. No artistic rendition could compete with this pageantry, and, after the last kiss and final blush of light, I would settle into a peek-a-boo game with the stars. This night was home to me, familiar, soothing, and just wild enough to keep me from straying too far from the farmhouse. Here awe and wonder rushed through me each night and I shivered as an awareness of God's omnipotence was thoroughly imprinted in me. My sense of my creatureliness was never far away, whether in sighting windstorms and sand gusts in the field, or when lapsing into breathless silence at the sound of the meadowlark at earliest dawn. God was always visibly "bigger" in this geography, and I was more than willing to enter into submission to and protection by that mystery.

In addition to these overtly sacred places, we may also have had special "safe" places where we could let our hair down, relax for a moment, and be ourselves. These places may have been hidden places, out of the way places, or reserved places where we alone could go. A favorite tree house, an overlook of grass, a special room in the house could be our sanctuary from the demands that life put on us. We felt protected there and able to let down inside. We may not have considered such places as especially significant in our spirituality, and yet they made it possible for us to learn how to be comfortable with ourselves and how to appreciate alone-time. In these spaces we could begin to know solitude as a formative experience.

I had three of these places that I can recall very readily. I was the eldest of five children and by the age of four I already felt like a little mother. There were two places in my family home where I could escape momentarily from my duties, both those that were self-imposed and those that were assigned by my mother. The first place was the bathroom, the only room in our house that had a lock on it. I could sneak in there, especially at night, curl up in my blanket next to the wall vent where heat flowed out in the cold winters of Montana, and feel incredibly comforted and embraced in warmth. No one would disturb me and I fantasized that the hot air coming up through the grate was God breathing warm consolation upon me.

The second place was under my brother's bed. It was a trundle bed, which when pulled out from the wall left a space underneath just big enough for a little person to crawl under. There was a night light plugged into the wall to ease my little brother's fear of the dark. Unconsciously, I connected that little light with the tabernacle light in church. I felt held and protected here, in a space that seemed sacred, special, and private. Here I could just be by myself and stoke my "familiarity" with the divine for a few moments.

The final safe place was my Nana's house. My maternal grandparents always showered me with affection, freedom, and acceptance when I visited them a couple of times a year. In their home I could surrender my "little mother" role and be the child that I missed being the rest of the time. I could play games, entertain my grandparents, and fritter away my hours without worrying about any reprimands or demands. At Nana's house I could be myself "age appropriately," free from concerns or cares. In her space I learned about a God who received me fully as a child, whether recalcitrant or responsive. My image of a gentle, receptive, and compassionate God was first born in her home.

Part of organic spirituality involves identifying the overlooked places where the mystery has been evoked in our lives. These are the places that still have the power to move us into a contemplative attentiveness. The sense of sacredness or safety they induced can continue to provide us with ongoing vitality for our spiritual lives. They can rekindle our natural ability to move into awe and cultivate wonder in everyday life.

We can all uncover hidden gems of wonder within the everyday places that we knew as children and within the places that we have come to know as adults. We may have added other spaces to the list of those from our childhood where God's nourishment has been felt. In pausing to reflect on these as adults, we can gain access again to their formative power for us and give ourselves the opportunity to rekindle some of the organic stimulation and comfort that these places provided for us in our youth.

Take a moment now to return to your story and ask:

> *Where were your sacred places as a child, places*
> *where you felt overwhelmed with an awareness*
> *of Something or Someone bigger than yourself?*

What places organically moved you to stillness and contemplation?

Where were the hidden places in which you could simply dwell with yourself and savor unfettered time, "merely being"?

What places in nature still drop you into an awareness of mystery and wrap you in awe and wonder?

Events: The Sacred Text of Our Lives

The scriptures of the major world religions articulate a story of relationship, its ups and downs, its fidelities and infidelities, especially those in relation to God. The scriptures are stories of individuals and peoples who fell down and who picked themselves back up, dusted off their knees, and proceeded again in the struggle. Some of these stories have been "canonized" for their significance. They form the written tradition which guides our religious heritage.

Many other stories will never merit that designation, but they can have the same kind of power and potential for instructing us on our path. Our stories may also be helpful to other people. The story of our struggle to be faithful to God can be formative for others as well as for ourselves when it is reflected upon.

Within organic spirituality, there are many hidden stories that carry the seed of the next stage in our spiritual maturation. The key is to take time to reflect upon the story and distill new meanings that lie nestled in the memories. As adults we can find new levels of significance that, prior to our reflection, were dormant. Part of the "work" involved in recovering this potency in our childhood is to become aware of organic stimuli that trigger associations and can help us recall incidents that lead to underlying connections.

I remember walking off the plane in Dar es Salaam, Tanzania, and feeling incredibly "at home" instantaneously. This was my first time in Africa and there was no logical reason for the sense of familiarity and ease that I felt. But it wasn't until nightfall that I made the first connection: the night sky and the heat of the savannah reminded me of summer nights on the farm in Montana.

I could have left the reflection there. I had surfaced one connection that served me in my adjustment process and I could have settled for that one gem. But, as time went on, I knew there was more to be gleaned from this association.

Several years passed and, on my return from Africa, I entered into a conversation with a colleague about places that evoke a sense of the presence of God. We were reflecting on the places that immediately drop us into an awareness of mystery and produce a sense of awe. Spontaneously, I blurted out, "Well, I know where that is for me. It is under the night sky." As I said these words, I knew that something powerful underrode my awareness. I began consciously to reflect on that "felt" awareness of God's presence. I knew that whenever I went for a walk at night under the stars, I automatically felt close to God. Slowly, as I went back in my mind to my earliest days when that presence was first felt, a rather fuzzy memory began to surface.

I was six years old and my mother had given birth to her fifth child in four years and suffered through two major surgeries. The demands of mothering were enormous, especially since at that time my father was working both on the farm and on the railroad. There came a point at which my mother was just overwhelmed. The decision was made to parcel out the five of us siblings to various relatives and friends for a time. I knew where I wanted to go. My Nana's house! But my maternal grandmother was more able to cope with the youngest children, so my twin sister and I, who were older, were sent to my paternal grandparents' home on the prairie. There were apples, homemade donuts, and great pancakes at this house. But there were few hugs, kisses, or condolences. This was an environment that, like the land around it, fostered stoic perseverance. So, with my best brave self in hand, I tried to comply.

I remember waiting in bed until I heard the breathing of my twin sister next to me become regular and quiet. As soon as she was asleep, I would let myself cry. My loneliness, my worry, and my pain could be expressed only here. One night, after she was asleep, I crawled onto the window sill above our bed and searched the flat dark horizon. I was looking for the headlights of my father's pickup, hoping that he might be coming to get us. But there was no solace in the land. I buried my face in my hands and cried some more.

Then, I looked up. To my six-year-old consciousness, it was as if that great black expanse of night hid two immense arms of comfort, which stretched around me and embraced me. The words that softly crept into my head were, "There, there. Go ahead and cry. It's all right. I'm right here." This was my first personal experience of the mystery as a consoling presence. As an adult, I later would come to call that mystery God. But right now it had no name. It was a presence that needed none.

While the specifics of the story may be embellished by time and reflection, the essence of the event remains the same: the meaning that I derived from that organically, if not consciously, was that the world was a safe place and Someone out there cared. Someone Big. No matter where I went, and no matter what happened, that night presence would "be there" faithfully. It formed a foundation of trust that allowed me years later to circle the globe alone but not lonely. A simple event, uncovered through gentle reflection and pondering, carried great significance and vitality.

Again, I invite you to pause for a moment of reflection. The memories of events like these can't be called up on demand, or by intense self-scrutiny. They surface gently. They are often triggered by physiological reactions that are subtle but carry greater weight than we might initially assume. Learning to take cues from our bodies is part of the gift of organic spirituality. Taking time to remember and dwell with the tragedies and triumphs of our childhood and adolescence can bring up new connections for our integration. Then, tragedies can actually be transformed into triumphs. My mother's illness was certainly a tragedy for me at six. But in my late thirties, reflection on the tragedy brought forth a foundational connection that continues now to feed my spiritual confidence.

A few questions for your reflection:

In the first ten years of your life, were there any significant events that you judge now to be tragic or triumphant in some way?

Can you slow down your recall of one of these events to plumb its depths further for meaning and spiritual significance? Did it teach you anything?

When did you first sense the world was safe or unsafe? What is the story around that?

*Looking back as an adult, what meanings can
you derive from one of the events?*

Things: Symbols and Sacramentals

We are tactile creatures. The things we see and touch can imprint our memories with associations and connections. Our capacity to reflect on our experience enables us to find meaning and create symbols for it. We can surround ourselves with the things that remind us of this meaning. Symbols can represent more in our own subjective memory than they might for another objective viewer. We invest them with potency.

We are taught this by those who go before us and give us messages about the symbols they hold important. As children, we take these symbols up in many ways and use them to form the foundation of our own spiritual base. Each religious tradition is rich in its own symbols that prompt a communal respect. These symbols connect individuals to one another. If they are effective, they also connect us to our own souls.

Families and households also have meaningful artifacts that tell stories and bring up memories. The pictures, music, religious articles, significant objects in our childhood environment all have stories behind them. They fill our treasure box of meaning to be unpacked in adulthood. Important images that can sustain our connection with those we love or admire can take on spiritual significance as we allow them.

My paternal Grandma's home on the prairie was filled with religious pictures and objects. Hers was a devout existence, expressed quietly but consistently by the framed photographs on her walls. Whether with a picture of Mother Cabrini, the children crossing a broken bridge with their guardian angel shepherding them, or the youthful head of Christ turned slightly in a circlet of gold light, she surrounded herself with reminders of holiness and piety. God was real, and recognized, and permeated her home.

Several hundred miles away, in my Nana's living room, a crucifix and a picture of the Blessed Virgin framed the two sides of a Maxfield Parrish print. "Daybreak" is a playful scene, rich in vibrant blues and greens. It illustrates an early morning encounter between two pubescent girls, one fully clothed in a toga-like sheath, reclining restfully beside a pool at the base of two Grecian pillars. The other young woman, totally nude, seems to have just emerged from the pool and is bent over in supplication to the other to join her. The ambiance of the entire photo speaks of freshness, cool vitality, and sexual ease.

The meaning I later articulated for myself in reflecting on the proximity of the Blessed Virgin to this provocative print was that all of this was of a piece, spirituality and sexuality, and it was okay to be embodied. Within this household there was a subtle blessing of our physical selves and our spiritual natures. Both had respect and a certain propriety in their coexistence. And one could be a little naughty and still be "spiritual."

In very different ways, my two grandmothers taught through their wall hangings a message about the world, God, and ourselves. Both grandmothers were very connected to the sacred and each of them symbolized it in the "things" with which they decorated their homes. Children growing up take symbols from the environment in which they live and integrate them in their own unique ways. In adult life they can utilize the symbols that were significant in their early days along with those appropriate for them in current times. "Things" of meaning can remind them of the sacred in the milieu within which they choose to live and instruct their own children.

Some questions for your own reflection on symbolic things in your life story:

> *What decorations attracted you in the homes you lived in as a child?*

> *What religious articles were important to those you loved and how did that affect you?*

> *As an adult, what formative (or deformative) associations do you now find in those images?*

> *What are five symbolic things you now possess that have spiritual significance to you?*

In Everyday Life

The last phrase in our definition of spirituality cannot be overlooked. Spirituality is a growing intimacy with God experienced through persons, places, events, and things *in everyday life*. This means that spirituality happens within the warp and woof of our daily routine, our everyday existence.

I am not in any way discounting the "va va voom" experiences that many of us have occasionally known. These "peak" experiences or "God-moments" can never be overlooked nor should their value be discounted. However, climactic events like St. Paul's conversion on the road to Damascus are usually extraordinary and memorable. Already they are somehow feeding our souls in our overt awareness of them as significant.

What we are interested in uncovering in this book are the hidden gems that are right under our noses but which have been ignored as not being spiritual because they did not carry the apparent punch that dropped St. Paul to his knees. These everyday experiences may lack drama, but they still hold power. It is in recovering some of these gentler, disguised sources of vitality that we may unleash some power and energy that could enliven our adult lives. While tornadoes, hurricanes, and volcanoes may be impressive, and they may be where we, like Elijah, expect to find God, it is often in the "tiny, whispering sound" that we may surprisingly hear the voice of mystery (1 Kings 19:12). At times it is the delicate encounters that give us the greatest nourishment.

In Summary

With this definition of spirituality, our entire lives take on new potential. The persons, places, events, and things of everyday life carry within them the seeds of great vitality. Our bodies carry in our cells the memory of organic catalysts for awe and wonder. Through reflection and gentle recall, the mentors of our awareness of the sacred can join the sacred circle of significant persons who both overtly and quietly shaped our spiritual formation. Places of wonder, places of safety and sacred mystery again can inspire and focus us on the divine. Triumphs and tragedies, reflected upon and integrated within the "bigger picture," can serve as a referent for ongoing gratitude and humility. Significant symbols can be reclaimed and added to the meaningful treasures that our adult story has amassed. New images and meanings can continue to emerge with ongoing pondering.

Organic Spirituality: What Is It?

Gina was getting baptized. Her baptism was to take place on a small peninsula at a youth camp where her parents had spent significant time with the staff. Religiously, this was an important day for her. Her parents were conscientious and they had spoken to her about this new life that she was being baptized into. Already at the age of five she knew there was something special going on.

But in addition to the wonder of all this attention, Gina was embraced by another wonder. It was an organic one. It was the week when the caterpillars had sluggishly taken over the property before their transition from fuzzy brown and black worms to breathtaking butterflies. Gina was smitten by these soft, slow-moving creatures.

She participated in the wonderful sacrament of inclusion and welcome at the water's edge. But as soon as the ceremony was over, she was off to explore other wonders. I watched her handle these small "moving pipe cleaners" with great tenderness and care. I saw her face rapt in wonder at this new life and I knew that she was beholding a miracle. She would grow intellectually to respect the sacrament she had just received, but the furry sacrament in her hand captivated her like nothing else could right now.

It is through Gina's five senses that she first discovers God. It is through her reaching out to touch, taste, smell, hear, and see the mystery of creation that she learns about a bigger mystery in the Creator. Gina is organically taken up with the wonder of a world that both excites and mystifies her. She does not have to understand it to take great pleasure in it. She simply opens up her hands and her heart and receives all that the Creator lavishes upon her. She delights in what comes naturally, and she revels in the discovery.

Organic spirituality refers to an awareness of the sacred that comes to us through a fundamental, integrated experience of mystery often experienced through our five senses. Webster's dictionary links the word "organic" to the phrases "relating to, or arising in a body organ; affecting the structure of the organism" and "forming an integral element of a whole: fundamental."[1] The definition of "organic" links the body to the formation of the person as a whole. The senses become "an integral element" in the shaping of our foundational selves, contributing to our spiritual identity and our sense of place in the world.

Throughout life, the five senses teach us about the larger world of which we are a part. Sense perceptions affect internal structure, and, when integrated into a whole, form the foundation which grounds our spiritual growth.

Among the many sources that contribute to the development of the spiritual life, I would like to name three for our consideration. These sources are organic, religious, and vocational. They are not mutually exclusive, and there may often be an overlap and interplay among them as a person integrates new information.

Let us take a closer look at each of these sources.

Three Spiritual Formation Sources: Organic, Religious, Vocational

In childhood we experience spirituality as one indivisible reality. At the center of our spiritual vitality is our capacity for awe and wonder. Without this, our interior dries up. Our imagination and our openness to "something more beyond ourselves" shrivel. It is our capacity for delight and surprise that enlivens our souls and allows God access to our deepest selves.

The first source of spiritual formation is organic in nature. It is through our embodied experience of awe and wonder that we discover the "bigger mystery" out there. Through our five senses, we touch, taste, smell, hear, and see a bigger world that fascinates us. We are taken up with the awesome fullness of this world into which we've been born. Often, this happens most obviously through the natural world. We glimpse something bigger than ourselves and we are attracted to it.

These attractions provide the context in which we reach for God. The hunger for "more" is embodied in a child's reaching out to touch and discover a larger world. We want that "more." We want to hold it in our hands and be filled with inspiration by it. This is our "transcendent dimension" through which our spiritual life takes its shape.[2] "Organic," then, refers to the spontaneous, sensory elements of our spiritual life that were most evident in unstructured experiences within our childhood. The transcendent dimension that opened up our spiritual lives was first experienced through our senses.

The second source of spiritual formation, a source that directly shapes us socially to fit into the larger human community, comes through tradition. Religious tradition introduces us to a vast amount of information which the human community has amassed in its attempts to explain the mystery. The collective wisdom, which many generations before have gathered and written down to instruct their children on how to respond to the mystery, is recorded in the scriptures of each religion. This body of wisdom forms the tradition on which our religions are based.

Initially, structured socializing occurs in our family. Each family has its own ethnic and historical tradition through which children are instructed about what life means. On a larger level, structured socialization occurs when we enter the institutions of our world, namely, school and church. It is in these communal venues that we learn that the mystery has a name. We are taught the name of the mystery in the appropriate forms that our social and religious communities have identified. "God" is catechetically and theologically introduced to us.

However, some of us never connect this catechetical notion of God with our felt experience of the mystery out there in the fields and forests of our childhood. There is often a gap. If we as children have no mentoring in how to deal with the conflict, the organic is often permanently disconnected from the religious. To alleviate the confusion felt between the wonder of the organic and the power of the tradition, we conform to social demands and we suppress the organic source of spiritual vitality. Developmentally, as we enter grade school, being accepted by our peers and adult authority figures becomes very important. We unconsciously make choices to let go of the organic aspects and focus on institutional adjustment.

Obviously, we need to learn some social disciplines to appropriately live in communal relationship with others. But spiritually, if the organic is completely overridden by religious routine, educational agendas, and cultural demands, the soul can be deformatively affected. We learn the rules, practice the disciplines, and perform the rituals, but we miss out on the reality that the organic and the religious can inform each other in a life-giving way. It is tragic when these two "goods" do not co-form each other naturally because they are not supported by knowledgeable authorities who recognize that both are important in spiritual formation.

In Gina's experience, organic elements of spirituality gracefully meet the religious tradition. Gina is touched literally by her furry friends, small, fragile creatures with whom she plays the happy caretaker. She is also touched by the worshiping community which bestows on her the promise to guard, protect, and take care of her in her religious identity. At this point there is no conflict for Gina, since those who surround her value both sources of spiritual energy in her spiritual formation. The tension emerges when the organic source is dismissed or replaced by religious concepts which do not inspire the child's consciousness. Adult mentors can assist children in negotiating this transition by revealing their own awe and wonder and by supporting the child in the cultivation of reverence and respect for mystery.

The third source of spiritual vitality is vocational. Sometime around the age of ten, the larger world begins to break in upon us and we feel a tug to somehow participate in it more fully and consciously. We are attracted to this larger world and to the human community that dwells in it. We want to participate more significantly in our world.

It is at about this time when we begin to ask ourselves the question, "What do I want to be when I grow up?" We want to join in the larger adult enterprise. If our souls are stirred in some way, our desire to give something back may shape our vocational choice. It is a very spiritual moment in which we decide what we want to do with our life energy.

At this point in our vocational evolution, a "fire" often ignites within us that moves us toward collaborating with something bigger than ourselves. This "original fire" erupts inside and may move us to ask how we can better serve others, the world, and God through our life work. It is often in this phase that religious vocations first are glimpsed, ministerial calls are first felt, and urges to serve the suffering in the world first emerge.

My own "original fire" was nourished by visiting missionaries coming home to share their stories of service in Brazil. A Jesuit priest from our parish showed his slides of the barrio where he had served. We would join together in a casual home liturgy around his mother's coffee table, then share a potluck meal together. I found my heart stirred by his stories and his example. I felt the first stirrings of a call to serve the poor viscerally rising up in my heart. I wanted to join others who hungered to make the world a better place. In my case, my church supported that fire, even though my calling mystified many in my family. For me, the organic influences melded well with the religious and vocational surgings; eventually I would act on that fire in responding to my vocational call to service in ministry.

When it comes to vocational discernment, the integration of the three sources may not be so simple. The organic and the religious can be stifled by cultural and familial pressures that push us away from our original fire of transcendent yearnings within. People sometimes choose a life work out of pragmatic, immediate, or ego-driven concerns, i.e., prestige, relational obligations, or economic advancement. Later in life, we may find ourselves regretting the loss of enthusiasm for the work to which we give ourselves daily. At mid-life, many of us bemoan the loss of the "original fire" that leapt within us in our youth. It may become necessary for us to reevaluate and perhaps consider other directions for our lives, directions which could bring fulfillment, express our heartfelt desires, and stretch us spiritually.

A Final Look at Organic Spirituality

If we lived in an ideal world, all three sources—organic, religious, and vocational—which influence our spiritual formation would be co-forming one another harmoniously throughout our lives. Organic influences would be allowed to flourish while being informed by religious tradition. Deformative religious elements would be identified and winnowed out so that more formative elements could constructively assist in our growth. Vocationally, the organic and the religious elements would coalesce gracefully with the urge to participate in the mystery and guide us to the vocation that is most congenial for our talents and aptitude. The spiritual aspect of our lives would be respectfully integrated into our life work.

Unfortunately, we do not live in a perfect world and this integration between the three sources is often delayed until adulthood. In fact, for many, the organic source may be entirely dismissed as invalid within an adult spirituality. The organic elements may go underground to survive the onslaught of religious and social influences. It is rare when all three of these elements fit smoothly with one another during the congested formation process from childhood to young adulthood.

The blessing is that, as adults, we can revisit these three sources to sort through that which is formative versus that which is deformative and rediscover those elements that may be hidden. With a mature mind and heart, infused by the Holy Spirit, we can discern which directives from the organic, religious, and vocational aspects of our lives are worth added attention. In the honest depths of our person, we know which of those directives are congenial for us and which are in sync with the divine. Organic spirituality does not mean taking all the impulses from our sensory perceptions and acting on them without reflection and prayer. Rather, it invites us to honor the contribution of our senses and memory and listen respectfully to the truth that can be found there. Discernment of the important messages from within our own interior is always a requisite for wisdom.

Discernment and reflection are necessary for our full recovery of soul and the integration of all aspects of our persons in relation to the divine. We can decide how to re-cultivate a rich sensory awareness that turns us toward the sacred. This recovery can revitalize our spirituality and re-fresh the religious practices that previously may have gone flat. It can also reinvigorate and clarify how our life work can become more life-giving and integral to our spiritual lives.

A reawakening of primal influences from childhood and youth, coupled with the natural awe and wonder experienced in adulthood, is what organic spirituality is all about. Developing a more reflective awareness of our stories and the significant pieces which lie within our dusty memories can help us understand the uniqueness of our lives. As we grow in our appreciation of the preciousness of everyday moments, we can begin to live with more attentiveness to the little gifts within the present moment.

The first part of this book has dealt with the importance of organic elements in the spiritual life. The theory needs a praxis, though. To concretely assist us in developing a more contemplative way of being, we will explore in the second part a sixfold path of organic spiritual practices which can help us in continuing our reflective process. These six spiritual disciplines can be applied in the organic reality of our everyday lives as busy adults. They can help us remain awake and present to the mystery around us and within us as we move around the circle of the sixfold path.

PART TWO
DISCIPLINES

An Introduction to a Sixfold Path

Four lean Asian figures stood poised in a semicircle in the park near my office. It was early morning and the traffic in the square was still light. I was stopped at a red light, waiting to turn left. They caught my attention because of their focused demeanor. Their hands were raised in relaxed circles above their heads and they stood very still. They did not move or shift their stance. There was no overt connection between them, but all of them radiated the same kind of attentiveness to their movement. Their stillness invited me to slow down, focus, and breathe.

Quietly, without words, their practice of T'ai Chi instructed me on my practice of the ancient spiritual discipline of stillness, one of the most difficult of these six practices for contemporary Westerners. However, equally alluring was the aura of solitude that surrounded them even as they moved in synchronicity with one another. The world around them was noisy and bustling. But within their still and focused rhythm, they were unperturbed by these externals. In the depths of their own persons, they had apparently tuned into a deeper

rhythm and were collaborating in dance-like gestures with it. This exercise did not result in isolation
or solipsistic individualism. It allowed them to enter
into a formative rhythm with themselves, their own
interior, and the divine. It facilitated their listening
to that still, small voice within them that oriented
and stabilized them for the day's journey ahead.

These people were putting into practice a daily
exercise that helped them develop a more contemplative consciousness. Deliberately, they were em-
ploying means from within one of the great religious
traditions to aid them in grounding themselves in
the mystery.

When we look at developing a more contemplative
awareness of the mystery of God in our lives, we may wonder
how it is possible to cultivate this within the complex reality
in which we live. How do we develop "the art and discipline
of presence to the Sacred"?[1] There are many spiritual practices and exercises that come from the great religious traditions of our world, but they may seem to require lifestyles
that do not fit our circumstances as parents, spouses, and active persons. Does that mean we cannot develop a more contemplative awareness of the mystery of God?

I would suggest that we have ample possibilities for raising our consciousness of God in an "organic" way within the
lives we lead. In the chapters that follow we will explore six
"organic" disciplines which may be helpful in fostering our
awareness of the sacred within busy lives. Together they
compose a sixfold path to a heightened awareness of God. A
few introductory remarks may be helpful.

First of all, we will explore these six organic disciplines
sequentially, but they could be viewed more accurately like

the ribs of an umbrella or the spokes of a wheel. Each of the spokes is independent, yet all are interconnected and anchored at the center. The overall strength of the wheel depends on the sturdiness of the individual spokes.

In the sixfold path toward a more contemplative consciousness, each of the six disciplines interrelates with the others. Much like the Eightfold Path of Buddhism,[2] these six organic disciplines support the practitioner's cultivation of awe and wonder. Practice of one will help in the practice of the others. All of them support our movement into the depth of who we are in relationship with God. The mastery of one is not necessary before the practice of the next begins. Conveniently, each of these "organic" disciplines begins with the letter "s." They are: slowing down, sharing our story, stillness, solitude, surrender, and solidarity.

Second, while there is no hierarchy among these disciplines, some are foundational. The foundational disciplines are necessary for the practice of the others. For example, we must slow down before we can experience stillness. As we examine the disciplines, we will indicate which ones are foundational.

Third, all six practices could easily be understood as "a simplifying process." Implied in each discipline is the gradual simplification of some aspect of life. All of them, therefore, are countercultural in a world that values complexity, speed, and productivity. These organic practices get us back to basics. Their purpose is the development of a contemplative way of being, an awareness of the sacred within and beyond us.

Fourth, none of these practices are new, but some of them have never specifically been identified as "spiritual disciplines." There may be reference to some form of these within the great religious traditions of the world, but several of the practices have never been articulated as having a benefit for our spiritual life.

To assist us in our own practice of the six disciplines, let us look at the obstacles that can impair our practice and the factors that can facilitate it. Circumstances and conditions within each of four distinct arenas can help or hinder our adjustment to the sixfold path.

Obstacles to and Facilitators of the Practice: Four Arenas for Awareness

Obstacles that block our practice and facilitators that enhance it can emerge from within any of the following four arenas: personal, familial, cultural, and ecclesial. When we begin to reflect upon and articulate our own story and our relationships, patterns emerge and connections can often be made that shed light on our attempts to deepen our practice of the sixfold path. Often we find that our practice is either hindered or helped by factors from within our past that might contribute to ease or discomfort with each of the disciplines. Awareness of these historical factors can prevent us from becoming overly critical of ourselves when we find a practice difficult.

The Personal Arena

This arena is unique to each one of us as individuals. Within our personal story and makeup, there may be factors that predispose us more readily to certain disciplines. Due to temperament, for instance, we may find ourselves naturally drawn to certain of the practices. We do not have to be limited exclusively to those practices toward which we gravitate,

nor need we feel controlled by those practices toward which
we do not gravitate. We can make adult choices about how
we integrate a practice given our limitations and aptitude.
Merely knowing of this tendency toward selectivity can raise
our awareness and inform our consciousness of what is required in our practice.

For example, I, personally, have a high metabolism. I
come by it naturally, for my mother also manifested it in her
youth. This physical attribute makes it hard for me to slow
down. Organically, I tend to move rapidly. My body operates
at a faster rhythm and I respond well to that kind of pace. It
is not unusual for me to climb the stairs two steps at a time.
This inheritance influences the way that I practice the spiritual discipline of slowing down. To a certain degree, I have
to apply extra attentiveness to my practice. I have to consciously remind myself that slowing down is something of
value in my spiritual life, and then build in external and internal verbal and visual catalysts that assist me.

Our personal idiosyncrasies, makeup, and history may
predispose us readily to some practices more than to others.
Our temperament may incline us toward certain disciplines
and impair us in our initial attempts to practice others. Keeping in mind our natural proclivities, we can help ourselves
recognize our strengths and challenge our areas of resistance.

The Familial Arena

Early in this book I mentioned some family patterns and
behaviors that have influenced me. Each of our family systems had patterns and behaviors that we imbibed organically
from childhood. We assumed that these patterns and behaviors were normative, that this was how all people lived their
lives. We may have been startled to discover that not every

family eats in silence, but that some families sit around the dining table and share stories of what happened that day. We may have come to realize that a whole set of assumed patterns was given to us, some of which may have been helpful to us in our spiritual formation and some of which may have hindered us. By becoming aware of these assumed patterns, we can demythologize them and broaden our choices for our own way of relating. This awareness can also help us understand our tendency to avoid certain disciplines if they were not encouraged in our family. The family's habits and styles of relating are ingrained within and need to be identified and reevaluated for a healthy way of living.

Here I mention again the significance of models for each of the six practices. In our homes we may have seen certain spiritual practices modeled by parents, relatives, and siblings. These mentors within our home life still have the power to influence our practice when our awareness of their impact is raised to consciousness. Raising our awareness can reinforce the formative effect.

As I mentioned earlier, I was the first of five children and my mother depended a lot on me to help her in the day-to-day routine in our household. For me, the atmosphere was frequently one of "red alert," living "on top" of things, always ready and responsive to the many needs around me. When it was time to go somewhere, the family dynamic was "Hurry, hurry. Don't dawdle. Let's get everyone in the car." That is what I tried to do as the eldest and that is what I was rewarded for. Here is another handicap in my practice of slowing down. I was rewarded for moving faster. It was interpreted as being responsible. To move slowly meant I was "lollygagging."

When I think of familial models for slowing down, I return again to my father. There was one speed when it came to my father: "his." It was consistent, methodical, and slow. He was true to his internal rhythm. When I was a child, it drove me crazy. My mother would say, "We're not going to open our Christmas gifts until your father has finished his bath." A groan would go up from all of us. We knew we had a good hour to wait. However, now that I am an adult, I appreciate the wisdom of that modeling in my family. He moved slowly and consciously. He modeled a contemplative pace. I now can return to that example to remind myself to slow down and become more attentive and focused.

Family dynamics can predispose us and reinforce deformative or formative living styles. If we name a habit or message that was coded into us from the arena of our family system, we can decode the influence that hampers our spiritual maturation. Again, raising it to consciousness, we can decide to re-pattern our behavior as adults who make choices and model this for our own children. Becoming aware of family biases and how these can impede the practice of these six disciplines is a great help in freeing us from assumptions that can thwart our practice.

The Cultural Arena

The larger social world in which we live continually feeds us clues about how to survive in our culture. We receive many subtle and overt messages, some of which uplift the spiritual life and others that detract from it. We imbibe these messages through osmosis by living in our world as social animals.

In his critique of contemporary culture, Ronald Rolheiser identifies certain factors that militate against the development of a "contemplative personality."[3] Attitudinal strains in our culture foster pragmatism, narcissism, restlessness, and individualism. These hinder our reflective capacities. Not surprisingly, our culture does not support the contemplative attitudes the six spiritual practices are meant to foster. Societal messages that compel us to "step lively," "get the job done," and "prove ourselves" are even more powerful if they have become part of our own value system. Cultural influences may combine with messages from the family and from our own makeup to make it triply difficult to practice certain disciplines.

We need to be aware of the cultural factors that affect our spirituality. For example, the cultural mandate of industrializing society is obviously opposed to the practice of slowing down. Such a practice is countercultural to all of the preferences of a culture that demands productivity, practicality, and speed. Success is measured in quantifiable terms and our striving to realize it is reinforced culturally by a pace that is non-reflective and hectic.

Much has been written about the toxic effect that hecticness has on the spiritual life. It may be necessary for us to stand up against this and other cultural biases for the sake of our spiritual formation. All of the six spiritual disciplines outlined in this book are countercultural responses to Western industrializing society. To practice these disciplines mindfully will entail a resistance to the cultural values that permeate much of our developing society.

The Ecclesial and Ministerial Arena

Some may find it surprising to realize that the church in her messages to the believing and ministering community may have less than formative influence, yet there are attitudes and schools of spirituality within our churches that inhibit our integration of a more contemplative approach to life. Some ecclesial attitudes and spiritualities that flow from pietistic or activistic perspectives can, in subtle ways, damage our practice of the sixfold path. It is equally damaging when the church applies to its members and ministers society's definition of "success" in terms of efficiency, quantity, and speed. If the church swings toward this type of self-assessment, it forfeits its prophetic mission of witness and defaults on its real gift to the world: awakening people to the sacred.

Many conscientious persons may find that a spirituality that supports overextension contributes to their fatigue and lack of inner groundedness. For example, a spiritual thrust toward perfectionism may underlie the push to "get it just right." Perfectionism often motivates our drive as parents, teachers, and pastoral associates. While this type of spirituality was promoted several decades ago, today we realize it may damage our capacity to surrender and assume a gracious, trusting stance in relation to the tasks and the timing of our lives.

This reality plays itself out in numerous ecclesial formats. Pastoral committees find themselves seduced by cultural biases in their attempts to overachieve. They sometimes are tempted to judge their effectiveness and success by the standards of the culture, rather than those of scripture. Parish teams discover that their time is scheduled away by meetings and agendas that have little directly to do with the gospel. Ministers feel pulled apart by projects with little time left for prayer and faith fellowship.

Those in ministry positions may find that ecclesial expectations and workloads hinder a call to form a more contemplative consciousness. Within an ecclesial milieu where the numbers of clergy are dropping, the needs of congregations are rising, and the cultural supports to deal with those needs are quite deficient, conscientious ministers may feel compelled to try to meet people's needs by overworking and overextending themselves. This attitude may be cloaked in spiritual language of apparent good. "Omniavailability"[4] is a primary danger for ministers and volunteers who try to be attentive and available to everyone, at all times, under all circumstances. It is dangerously reinforced by scriptural interpretations which encourage leaders to "be like Jesus," accessible by all the people all the time. These interpretations often ignore the many times when Jesus went away to pray in a remote place and restore his sense of the sacred.

All this places the church at an extremely dangerous junction. The foundation that the church offers to society is in the realm of the spiritual life. If ministers themselves cannot realistically foster their own contemplative consciousness, they will be unable to help anyone else to do so, much less contribute to the transformation of the larger world.

While we have focused on hindrances, we can also find in each of these four arenas factors that support a contemplative way of being. Within our personal temperament, our family systems, our societal milieu, and our church community, many formative supports are present to assist us in our spirituality. Becoming aware of these supports and tapping into them can help us to maximize our energy in practicing each of the six disciplines. Naming the source of support can also be a help whenever we need extra confirmation.

Let us move on now to examine each of the disciplines of the sixfold path to contemplative consciousness.

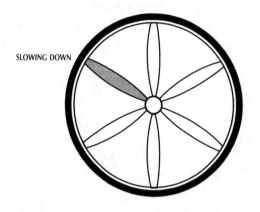

SLOWING DOWN

SLOWING DOWN

I used to work in a building that was the length of a football field. The office where I gave spiritual direction was at one end of the building and the office where a staff telephone was available was at the other end. Periodically, I would need to make a time-sensitive call between sessions. I became very crafty at designing ways in which I could sprint the length of the hall, make a telephone call, and sprint back within ten minutes.

The real challenge often was not the sprint or the call; it was arriving in a recollected way to meet my next directee. I remember several times when, while I was darting down the hall in true Olympic form before my next appointment appeared, someone would stop me and challenge me to "practice what I preach."

"You talk all about 'slowing down,' Nicki," they would say, "but you move so fast." It was a clarion call to reevaluate my circumstances and approach.

Even though there is no hierarchy among the six organic disciplines, slowing down is primary. It is one of the most foundational practices of the sixfold path. It is also one of the most difficult. Moving rapidly is imprinted upon us early in our lives by family, culture, and education. An association between moving fast and getting something done is reinforced on many levels. The message we receive throughout our schooling, our athletic training, and our professional preparation is "Fast is good." To go against this is to challenge some of the most basic orientations of our contemporary society.

The Spiritual Benefits of Slowing Down

What is the spiritual value of the practice of slowing down? How is it that we can call this a "spiritual discipline"? What are the benefits involved?

The first spiritual benefit of slowing down can be stated simply:

SLOWING DOWN FACILITATES INTIMACY.

To ground ourselves, let us return to our original definition of spirituality. If spirituality is a growing *intimacy with God*, experienced through persons, places, events, and things in everyday life, then we have to look at what fosters intimacy. Because "intimacy with God" requires an awareness of the presence of God, slowing down is essential.

Slowing down facilitates intimacy in its many forms and allows for the disengaging from preoccupations that prevent reflectiveness. Did you ever attempt to intimately engage with someone when they were moving fast? A rapid pace inhibits intimacy. It frustrates the connecting process that is essential to intimacy. Intimacy requires some deliberate, focused attentiveness to the other.

In order to focus and zero in spiritually on the One with whom we would be intimate, we must slow down. The first spiritual benefit, then, of slowing down is that a slower pace makes intimacy possible.

SLOWING DOWN IS AN ESSENTIAL PRACTICE
FOR SPIRITUAL MATURATION.

According to the contemplative tradition within all the major world religions, slowing down is an essential element in spiritual maturation. While the phrase "slowing down" may not appear in a religion's formal instructions for spiritual growth, it is a precursor to all spiritual practices.

None of us can deny the natural slowing down process that occurs with physical aging. Many of us know wise old men and women whose opinions we highly value because they have reflected on life and integrated well the lessons they have learned. These "wisdom figures" have matured in age and grace, and they share with us the benefits of their insight.

Within the spiritual life, the aging process is respected and seen as conducive to integrating the experiences of life. We do not have to wait until we are elderly to begin this integration, however. We can change our life rhythm to a slower pace to assist this integrative process. Consciously, we can build in opportunities for reflection and integration when we alter our life rhythm.[1]

This brings us to our third spiritual benefit.

SLOWING DOWN REINFORCES A GENTLE PACE CONDUCIVE FOR DEEPER REFLECTION.

Reflection requires a gentle pace, internally and externally. Gentleness is a disposition that is rare in many of our lives. Taking a gentle approach toward our world and ourselves may not be something we were ever encouraged to do.

Many of us may be more familiar with a critical approach to reflection than a gentle one. Reflection for us may connote evaluation, scrutiny, and critique. We may not have had much experience in appraising our way of living gently. This artful approach to appraising life requires patience, self-presence, and honesty.[2] Incorporating a gentler approach to reflection can involve the supportive practices of abiding, attentiveness, and remaining awake. Carolyn Gratton speaks of this trifold discipline as the preparation for entering a deeper level of life review.

When we abide with another, we are present to that person. We remain with that person, fundamentally open and receptive. Abiding in the Spirit means dwelling with gratitude in an attempt to be present to God. This allows us to grow in our attentiveness to God, even when there are changes in our lives. We continue to trustingly focus on God within the ambiguity of change. Finally, this attentiveness awakens us within. Something is opened up intuitively for our consideration, and this something can lead us to our true self. We are aware on a deeper level. We want to remain awakened to the mystery that leads us to a more authentic connection with ourselves.

The process of abiding, attending, and remaining awake with God facilitates a gentler rhythm of life through which we can recognize and more readily receive the small gifts of God and integrate them within ourselves.

We come now to the fourth spiritual benefit of slowing down:

SLOWING DOWN ALLOWS US TO FINE-TUNE OUR AWARENESS
OF THE SHIFTS OF HEART THAT COULD AID
OUR SPIRITUAL WELL-BEING.

Slowing down is vital for fostering the capacity to notice the external details of our world and the internal movements of our own selves. It is much easier to take notice of different movements inside us when we are not rushing around. Like fine-tuning a radio to a particular frequency, we need to fine-tune our inner attentiveness to God's call for our growth and change. Listening carefully and adjusting the process we use to get the best reception require a slowed, deliberate, and attentive presence.

I remember one time when I was bustling around in the kitchen. I was putting the clean dishes away and making considerable noise while doing so. My husband appeared at the doorway and watched me for a few minutes. Then, quietly, he asked, "Honey, do you have a headache?"

I grumbled a little and then paused to answer his question. "Well, now that you mention it," I answered, "I do. Why do you ask?"

"Because," he said "you always seem to move faster when you don't feel well."

I was stopped short by his observation. He was right. I accelerated when I was in pain in order to "get everything done" so that I could then, without guilt or worry, rest and recreate a bit. He had noticed the correlation before I had and he raised my awareness.

Slowing down allows us to perceive feelings, pain, and discomfort in order to tease out what those experiences are "telling" us. We can then choose a response that will be more conducive to our spiritual welfare. The practice of slowing down can help us become more attuned to God who may be inviting us to shift our patterns of behavior. We examine our consciousness to see how it is aligned with God. We can then make changes to restore our contemplative connection with ourselves, others, and God.

These are only four of many benefits that come to us with the practice of slowing down. The next step in the process is to identify the means that we can use to practice this spiritual discipline. How do we actually practice "slowing down"? Let us look at two forms.

The Practice of Slowing Down: External and Internal Forms

Slowing down as a spiritual discipline can be practiced externally as well as internally. Both forms involve a simplifying within our lives that carries certain ramifications. Externally, each act requires a reduction in the glut of stimuli to which we subject ourselves, whether that means turning off the radio when we go to work or limiting the amount of time we spend in front of the television. Internally, we may also need to simplify the expectations that we place upon ourselves by limiting the number of tasks we plan to complete in a day or in an evening. This may entail scaling down our striving for accomplishment.

Slowing down in its external form is an obvious discipline of the body. This is important for us as Christians. Our theology of incarnation recognizes the amazing miracle of

God becoming human in Jesus Christ. The historical reality of divinity slipping into human flesh should transform our attitude toward our own bodies. Divinity saw flesh as good enough to dwell in. That means that our own bodies carry a certain innate blessedness. They are temples for the divine.

Are our bodies really temples? Do we respect our bodies enough to listen and attend to them? Are we willing to slow down enough to take stock of the whispered messages our bodies give us with regard to health, well-being, and spiritual attentiveness?

As illustrated in the story above, my body was giving me clues to which I did not want to attend. I had my functional agenda: get these dishes put away and get the kitchen in order. *Then*, I could relax. But my body was indicating how rest was needed much more immediately than I wanted to admit. My coping mechanism was to move faster. The pace by which I was finishing my task was a rushed camouflage for my desire to force my own agenda. I had blocked my own awareness of pain in order to achieve that.

The external practice of slowing down honors God in the flesh. It incarnationally attunes us to a bigger reality. Our personal rhythms are synchronized harmoniously within a bigger movement. We can gauge our practice of slowing down externally by the rate at which we move our bodies. Our application of slowing down is tested every day in the way in which we live in our flesh.

Slowing down is a physical discipline in which the contributions of our physical body are respectfully taken into account in an integration process. This change in our pace can raise our conscious awareness of internal messages that have to do with our own spiritual unfolding. Slowing down can focus us on a deeper sense of direction, purpose, and participation within the cosmos. We can get in touch with our own organic rhythm from which we may be distracted by the external world. Without this discipline, we run the risk of being permanently manipulated by the pace of industrializing society, without a conscious base from which to appraise our responses.

Our external practice of slowing down is more easily measured than our internal practice, but often the two are connected. The superabundance of external stimuli from our world is difficult enough to deal with, but at times of crisis it can be compounded by an eruption of internal clamor. At such times our healthy, spiritually grounded response requires more focused, deliberate attentiveness. To foster tranquillity in the midst of tremendous change, for instance, we need to be sensitive to the need for a calm interior with which to receive the world and its complexity while maintaining some inner balance. Times of transition will demand more psychic energy. A slowed down rhythm will help us to cope more authentically and more gracefully.

Our internal practice of slowing down faces us with the underlying question, "Why do we go fast?" Some of us might answer that question by citing the demands of the culture. We are compelled to go fast to succeed, to finish our work, to get ahead. These are very real external pressures.

But sometimes there are equally compelling internal pressures. The demands within ourselves may be pushing us to move rapidly. Inner compulsions, fears, and the desire to avoid the pain inside ourselves may combine with the external pressures and reinforce our rapid lifestyle. Sometimes we go fast because of inner anxieties and expectations that are exacerbated by societal demands. Or we go fast to avoid the internal congestion of the unresolved issues of our lives.

Many times, in spiritual direction, people will complain that they cannot slow down. "When I slow down," they say, "all this stuff comes up." That is exactly the inner work to be done, sometimes in spiritual direction or therapy. This is the internal congestion that needs its day in the sun. It is made up of hidden internal pressures that inhibit inner stillness and propel us into seeking a fast escape. Unless we address these internal fears, slowing down will be fraught with tension and resistance.

Culturally, we will find little support for slowing down to facilitate spiritual development. Belden Lane reminds us that

> to move slowly and deliberately through the world, attending to one thing at a time, strikes us as radically subversive, even un-American. We cringe from the idea of relinquishing in any moment, all but one of the infinite possibilities our culture offers us. Plagued by a highly diffused attention, we give ourselves to everything lightly. That is our poverty. ...One can love only what one stops to observe.[3]

In contrast, many wise persons before us learned to take time to attend to the minute details of life, paying attention respectfully to the hidden directives from God within them. Radical simplicity experienced in a slowed down reflective life strips away nonessentials and allows us to focus our attention in order to receive and relish the insights of a life lived gracefully. The spiritual practice of slowing down can assist us in tempering the anxiety that causes us to move fast. It can provide a gentle space, a place in which we can calmly unfold our story and reflect in a more genuine, contemplative way. From there, life looks different and we can more readily hear the voice of God within.

Questions for Our Practice of Slowing Down

As we close this chapter, a few questions may help us assess and improve our ability to slow down externally and internally. Practiced consciously, slowing down can greatly in-
crease the quality of life and the depth of awareness of the
sacred within everyday life. Becoming aware of how we can
slow down will prepare us well for the development of the
other five spiritual practices in the sixfold path to contemplative consciousness.

> *On an external level, how fast do you eat? How
> fast do you walk? Shower? Shave? Drive?*

> *Is your body moving too fast and, therefore, pre-
> venting you from breathing, relishing, and sa-
> voring?*

> *Where can you already identify healthy patterns
> of slowness that help you foster your awareness of
> the sacred?*

> *Realistically, what is one rhythm that you could
> slow down?*

> *Internally, what interior work do you need to do
> to clear up some of the congestion? Spiritual direc-
> tion, counseling, journaling, or a support group?*

> *What compels you to move rapidly?*

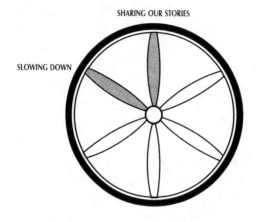

SLOWING DOWN

SHARING OUR STORIES

I was on my way to Africa to serve as a lay mission-
ary. There were troubles in the country to which I
had been assigned and I had been asked to wait in
Europe until it became safe for me to enter my mission site.

In the meantime, it was decided that a visit with
some of the elderly confreres who had served overseas would be advantageous. I sat at the dining table
with several retirees who had served in central Africa
and I began to ask them about their experience as
missionaries.

Many of these men were in their eighties, and it
was phenomenal how they perked up in response to
my questions. They began to tell me the stories of
how they had traveled by boat in the early days from

Holland to Africa and built churches, schools, and mission compounds. Out came the stories of snakes and spiders, lengthy walks in the sun, and survival in the most difficult of circumstances. They grew more and more animated as they dipped back into their memories and spread out the script of how they had endured struggle for the sake of the gospel and their vocation.

I sat there amazed. Their stories were rich and earthy and full of humor. These men inspired me. I found myself reflecting on the untold wealth within each of them. Hidden in their collective memory was a fantastic tale of daily fidelity to God in the face of incredible odds. I wished I could record a chronicle of their lives so that the people of my generation and those after me could benefit from their experience, their wisdom, and their joy.

This was a formative goldmine. In sharing their stories they stimulated reflection on my own choice and helped me feel buoyed up in readiness for my own departure for Africa.

The second organic spiritual practice in the wheel of the sixfold path we are circling is that of sharing our stories. Our story is the sacred text of how God is revealing God's self to us. As stated earlier, it is in the events and movements of our story that meaning is derived and wisdom becomes possible.

Many of us would not readily view sharing our story as being a particularly spiritual practice. Yet, the more we allow ourselves to drop into our own experience as human beings, the closer to sacredness we get. In our stories are the issues of life and death, struggle, the hunger for safety, faith, hope, and love. These are primal issues that form our experience of ourselves in relationship with other people and with God. These experiences instruct us on the value of remaining faithful and persevering in the journey of spiritual intimacy with God.

In many ways, our holy scripture is an extended story of the fidelity of groups of believers in relationship with God. The stories within the canonical text of the Bible are enduring tales of human beings trying to figure out the messages of God within the reality of their lives. These stories were powerful enough to be written down so that subsequent generations could learn from their ancestors' struggles of faith.

Our own stories carry some of the same potential and power. In the sharing of our stories we can reflect on our own experience and glean valuable insights for our own lives as well as for the benefit of others.

The Spiritual Benefits of Sharing Our Stories

What are the benefits of the organic spiritual discipline of sharing our stories? Although there are many important spiritual benefits that this discipline can offer to us and to others, let us focus here on three of those benefits.

IN SHARING OUR STORIES, WE PARTICIPATE IN HISTORY
AND THE TRANSMISSION OF FAITH
TO THE NEXT GENERATION.

The notion that in sharing our stories we contribute to history may sound somewhat grandiose. Yet, in the telling of our stories we pass on the tradition of our attempts to be faithful within the context of the age in which we live. We offer our own insights about the journey of faith to present and future generations.

Human beings are social creatures. Our lives are unique, but they are communal as well. We depend on the insights of those who have gone before us to instruct us. From them we can learn ways and means not only for survival but also for moving toward optimal health and happiness. Other people's discoveries can inform us about shortcuts and alternative routes that have been tried successfully. They can also warn us of dangers along the path.

When we hear other people's stories and tell our own, we often discover companionship in our vulnerability. We connect with each other through that vulnerability and bond with one another. We discover that we are not the only ones who have suffered. Personal storytelling may serve as a check-and-balance for our perceptions of being alone in the world with our troubles. A new form of solidarity can emerge. We may even be able to contextualize our struggle within the broader historical struggle in the human family, the church, and the world.

In this light, our stories take on new importance. We become bridge figures through which the faith of past generations is transmitted to those in the future. Our stories link generations as we contribute our insights of "living a life" to the evolutionary body of wisdom offered to those who come after us.

Perhaps we cannot clearly demonstrate the ways in which the next generation will be deprived in some way if we refrain from speaking our experience. Yet, subtly, there is a benefit to each voice's expression and reception. When we share our stories, we add our own voices to the whole body of souls who have gone before, and we participate in the development and transmission of a wisdom that is evolving with each life lived.

SHARING OUR STORIES CULTIVATES HONESTY.

When we tell our stories aloud, a new level of intimacy with ourselves opens up. We hear ourselves tell the story and explain the motives and movements that have shaped our decisions in life. In the telling, we own the story on another level. The images and memories no longer lie dormant inside.

As we frame the little stories within the large story of our lives, we can see how specific situations fit into the entirety of our spiritual unfolding. A reflective process can accompany the telling, allowing us to behold in a deeper way the individual vignettes within the broader framework of our lives. This gives us the opportunity to assess the truth more clearly. We can remove the camouflage we live under and become more honest about the underlying desires of our hearts. This self-knowledge can help us assess the choices that we have yet to make within our lives. Illuminated with an awareness of our own story, we can check these decisions for their consonance with the rest of our story. We can integrate our insights into how we have lived and benefit from them in the way we make decisions in the future.

The second benefit is directly connected to the third:

SHARING OUR STORIES RENEWS HUMILITY.

In the classical literature on the spiritual life, the renewal of humility is always highly valued. When we share our stories, we renew our humility in two ways.

First of all, in the telling, we can often see patterns and pitfalls within our lives. Knowledge of vulnerabilities can help us to more gracefully assume personal responsibility for the strengths and weaknesses that are part of our makeup. We become less likely to blame outside realities for that which is really of our own choosing. Humbly, we can come to accept the full spectrum of our personhood.

Perhaps, too, we may find that in the telling our darkness begins to look different to us. The new light that is shed can move us toward greater self-acceptance. Perfection seems less important as we start realizing that we are loved by God as we are, a mix of warts and wonder. A certain levity can emerge that allows us to see amusing challenges in the midst of our darkness. Taking ourselves less seriously can be a great gift that adds perspective to a self-critical tendency. A renewed sense of our creatureliness can restore a humility which is spiritually helpful in our maturation process.

The awareness of these patterns and pitfalls also forearms us for subsequent decision making. It equips us with a self-knowledge that can warn us and instruct us when similar situations arise in the future. Forewarned is forearmed. We can be pro-active in preventing ourselves from falling into a habit that may not be life-giving. We may discover blockages to which we had previously been blind. Stilted attitudes and dispositions may appear that take on new significance and require additional reflection. They may need to be refined or corrected to become more harmonious with what we say we want to be as spiritual human beings.

Second, our humility is renewed when we share our stories with others because we enter into a forum of accountability in the telling. We risk intimacy with those to whom we disclose our stories. We invite them into our lives, giving them permission to witness our vulnerability with us. To a certain degree, we give them permission to help us see where we can grow. "Can you help me out here?" we ask them. "Help me see where I cannot."

A word to listeners may be appropriate here. In the intimacy of the sharing of stories, we step onto holy ground. God's revelation is spelling itself out for the one who speaks and for the one who listens. Those who behold this revelation are asked to remove their shoes and honor the sacred space that is created in the telling. Judgment has no place here. Listeners become the face of God for the speaker in this intimate encounter. With the same compassion and care that God would offer, listeners can give feedback about what they hear. The speaker is transparent before them and God. This transparency can lead to a profound experience of humility and transformation for both the speaker and the listener. It is a circumstance of intimate investment by the speaker and requires the respect and reverence that such a trust deserves.

We can easily see how the sharing of our stories contributes to the transmission of the faith tradition, cultivates honesty, and renews humility. How do we practice this delicate discipline so that it becomes formative for us?

The Practice of Sharing Our Stories

There are a number of venues for a quality experience of sharing our stories. Within the various religious traditions, rich examples abound of persons who sought out direction from wisdom figures whom they trusted. Some of them, like Nicodemus, went under cover of darkness to have a private conversation about the direction of their lives of faith. Others, like the desert fathers and mothers, sought direct input from sages with whom they shared their temptations and perceptions.

Whether we are in crisis or mere confusion, there are helpful listeners with whom we can unpack our stories and tease out meaning. Traditionally, spiritual directors and confessors have been a great support. Today, formation counselors and therapists can aid in helping us understand the movements of our lives, in seeing the blockages, and in dealing with the deformations that may dispose us toward repeating mistakes. Small groups like support groups and spiritual direction groups can also provide a safe environment in which to disclose and process the challenges of life. Solid friendships with others who are grounded in faith and open to the Spirit can provide the opportunity for confidently sharing our story and receiving feedback.

The reality is that the sharing of our story is as ongoing a spiritual practice as is the first discipline of slowing down. It is not accomplished in one sitting, one seminar, or one year. Most of us can benefit from having at least one trustworthy person with whom we can share the whole of our story.

Dorotheus of Gaza, a third-century desert father, affirms that each of us needs someone who knows our story in its entirety to help us discern more carefully the movement of the Spirit within us. He states that "we should not believe that we can direct ourselves. We need assistance, we need guidance in God's grace."[1] When we consult with our confidante, that person can prevent us from deceiving ourselves about the direction of our lives. He or she helps us to remain honest and stay the course which will lead us to becoming our true selves.

Interestingly enough, our story can be told many times and generate new meaning in each retelling. New insight can be gleaned, because each time we tell the story, we reframe it in a new light and give it new meaning. If we have integrated the insights from the last telling, certain aspects of the story may shift. A new emphasis may appear, a new significance may emerge, and the event may re-write itself in our memory.

The opportunity to share the story of our struggle within the context of our whole life provides us with two benefits. It enables us to:

(1) note personally the consonance of the current individual struggle with the entirety of our whole story in the presence of a trustworthy other, deriving new meaning and insight from the telling, and

(2) experience the welcoming and challenging support of intimacy with another person with whom we share.

Thus, two forms of intimacy are fostered in the sharing of our story: intimacy with ourself and intimacy with another. Both of these facilitate a growth in our capacity to enter into deeper intimacy with God and enhance our spiritual life.

The sharing of our story is a valuable practice in helping us develop a more reflective way of living. It provides interpersonal feedback from someone we trust. The person who hears our story can model compassionate ways for us to receive our own story and adapt our narrow perceptions to a larger reality that we may previously have been unable to glimpse. The listener can teach us how to bring to light the stories that we were perhaps afraid of and allow them to be defused of their power. Even the stories that we fear to tell can be infused with new meaning and integrated into our spiritual lives.

Questions for Our Practice of Sharing Our Stories

Sharing our stories may come more readily for some than for others. It is a spiritual practice that requires trust and reflection as we move out of our isolation into intimate relationship with another person. Hearing our own voice tell the story, reflecting on it with another caring person, and teasing out the ramifications of the events can greatly broaden our understanding of our lives. Spiritually, we invite another into this sacred space and allow that individual's input and insight to complement our own. Persons, places, events, and things that previously lay hidden can take on new significance as they are revealed in the storytelling. New connections can be made that can inform a healthier approach to conflict, stress, or survival. These insights can help guide our spiritual search.

In combination with slowing down, sharing our stories can introduce a new level of awareness and wisdom for living life. For many of us, these are uncharted waters, rich with raw material for development and refreshment. Through writing, speaking, and disclosing, sharing our stories becomes a bountiful discipline with great spiritual potential.

Take a few moments now to consider the following questions for your own reflection about the practice of sharing your story as a spiritual discipline.

Where do you share your story?

Where do you share your whole story?

Are there stories within your life that you tend to leave at the door of the church, expecting them to be unacceptable for your spiritual process?

Would sharing your story be most comfortable with a spiritual director, a therapist, a support group, or a friend?

What inhibits you from taking the risk to share your story?

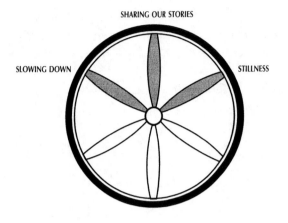

SHARING OUR STORIES

SLOWING DOWN

STILLNESS

STILLNESS

It was Christmas evening. All the packages had been
opened, the dinner had been eaten, and we were
stuffed with Christmas turkey. We had spent the day
with our adopted family playing board games and
watching seasonal television programs. The atmosphere was one of contentedness and calm as the last
strains of the closing music from "A Charlie Brown
Christmas" faded. All four adults had settled into
comfortable chairs. The three boys, age fifteen, twelve,
and nine, had stretched out on the carpet in front of
the Christmas tree. When the youngest got up and
climbed into his mother's lap, she put her arms
around him and said quietly to her husband, "Turn
out the light." He reached over and clicked off the
lamp nearest him and we all paused in the glow of the

illuminated Christmas tree. No words were spoken. Everyone sat quietly and reverently before the symbol of the season, bathed by its gentle light. We all paused to savor the final moments of this most precious day. For fifteen minutes or more we basked in stillness and refreshed our hearts with its taste and its feel, embraced by the solitude, yet together, touching the sacred that is bigger than each of us.

In her decision to turn out the lights, my friend was teaching her sons a very important lesson. She was modeling the spiritual practice of stillness, inviting them to pause in the activity of the day and reconnect with something bigger.

I smiled afterward at the simplicity of the act. She may not even have realized how formative an instruction it was. I was taken by the ease with which her children entered into the silence and stayed with it. It is a discipline that many young people long for, having spent many of their school days as latchkey kids with a television set for a babysitter. My friend was instructing her children on a mystery and giving them permission to turn off the stimuli of society and savor the simple, the quiet, the sacred. Through that Christmas experience, they all tasted something so sweet: the stillness of their own beings in the mystery of the moment.

This event may not seem particularly spiritual, yet such an everyday experience has the power to school each of us in the practical knowledge of stillness. This particular spiritual practice is badly needed, as so many people lack the basic internal dispositions and means to linger in a purposeful and focused way.

There is a reason why I have deliberately chosen the word "stillness" instead of the word "silence." Think about how many of us grew up with a punitive experience of the word "silence." "Be quiet!" we may have been told by annoyed parents and teachers. "Sit down, and shut up." It rings with retribution and reprimand.

Stillness, on the other hand, is free of those associations for most of us. It is a softer word that connotes presence rather than absence. Stillness is a holistic state of being rather than a mere lack of sound. To be still requires more than just silence. It requires a complete investment of self and a cessation of inner clamor as well as external noise. In fact, some of us have experienced stillness even in very noisy contexts. It can be "happened onto" when we are attentive and open. Stillness is actually an interior quality that spreads out to embrace the whole of us.

For me, therefore, stillness is a better term. It is the experience of fullness within emptiness, a paradoxical relaxation in expectancy. We can sense the sacred mystery in our very breath. Often it is a surprise experience of grace, given when we least expect it. It is a glimpse of something much bigger than ourselves, something that we cannot force but toward which we can only orient ourselves in readiness and willingness.

The Value of Stillness as a Spiritual Practice

There are many reasons why stillness can benefit us spiritually. Let us look at four of them.

IN STILLNESS, WE SIMPLIFY OUR INTERIORS
AND GET UNDERNEATH THE NOISE TO WHAT IS ESSENTIAL.

As I mentioned earlier, each of these organic spiritual practices involves a simplification process. In the practice of stillness, we let go of the cushion and trappings of stimuli and drop down into an emptiness which is life-giving. This emptiness can teach us. It can clarify for us what is important for us and give us a refreshed, clean view of our everyday lives.

In the practice of stillness, we intentionally limit the stimuli that distract us from this emptiness. We choose to turn off the radio in our cars as we drive to work and we give ourselves the joy of the quiet. Brother David Steindl-Rast speaks of the inference we make when we use the term "take a rest" or "take a walk."[1] There is a certain "grabbiness" implied in the "taking." How different it is to "give ourselves to" something; it changes the entire disposition by which we live life. It is gentler, more open, and more receptive. It is freer. Rather than taking control of the activity, we allow ourselves to savor it. In many ways, "giving" ourselves a space of quiet allows us to practice a receptive way of being, which is a prerequisite for a contemplative consciousness.

IN THE PRACTICE OF STILLNESS AS A SPIRITUAL DISCIPLINE,
WE LEARN TO WAIT MORE GRACEFULLY.

Waiting is hard for many of us. Our fast-paced world with all its demands does not encourage waiting. Waiting is not valued in a highly mechanized culture. We seem to feel put upon if we have to wait for a bus or we find ourselves sitting anxiously when there is a backup on the turnpike.

Waiting is important in the spiritual life. So much of our spiritual development in relation to God occurs through God's initiative. To a certain degree, we are at God's mercy. God can reach out in any way at any time that God chooses. We, on the other hand, must wait for that "stirring of the water" that occurs in the gospel (John 5:4). To be ready to immerse ourselves in God when God beckons, we must develop our capacity to wait.

There are many ways of waiting. There is the "pacing-waiting" of someone awaiting the return of a loved one from surgery. There is the waiting that goes on in a dentist's office. How do we usually find ourselves waiting in these everyday situations? Medical studies have tuned into the long-term side effects of waiting in anxiety. People who sit habitually on the edge of their chairs, as if, by being alert in readiness, they could push the clock ahead, may incur stress-related illnesses of the heart, vascular system, and muscles.

These are anxious forms of waiting that reflect a desire "to take charge" in a controlling way. There are other forms of waiting that are conducive to deepening our spiritual life. These forms involve a waiting that is tranquil, open, and receptive. They are forms that enable us to breathe and allow for God's surprises. People who wait gracefully use moments of delay as opportunities to cultivate awareness of mystery and awe. They allow themselves to grow in their capacity to wait graciously in anticipation of God's visitation.

In the practice of stillness as a spiritual discipline, we wait. We still our souls. We become attentive to something bigger. When we practice this discipline, we are deliberate and focused. In this still, open space, God can speak. Transformative intimacy is possible. An encounter with God can occur. Our spiritual life deepens and we mature in our capacity to attend to the God who comes.

WHEN WE PRACTICE STILLNESS AS A SPIRITUAL DISCIPLINE,
WE CAN APPRECIATE MYSTERY FROM A BIGGER PERSPECTIVE.

When we drop down into that still space or we are brought there by the surprise of God, suddenly a new horizon opens up for us. We cross a threshold in consciousness that allows us to see a bigger picture of which we had previously been unaware. Things look different in this moment of awe. A sunset catches us by surprise in its beauty and we see a bigger reality.

In stillness, we experience awe. We take it in. As we absorb what we behold, our natural response is one of humility and reverence. The mystery is so much bigger than our own perception and, when we glimpse it, it radically shakes our assumptions and our priorities. We know Who that Mystery is and we can only assume a stance of wonder before it. But we are attracted to what we experience and we want more.

The practice of conscious stillness stretches us in our capacity to retain that glimpse. We stretch in our ability to remain in that bigger mystery and sustain our awareness of it in the in-between times of normal consciousness. We taste that largeness of life and it feeds us.

The practice of stillness predisposes us for humility and reverence. It prepares us internally for that sense of oneness with God that we periodically experience. While it is not a guarantee of any "razzmatazz" experience of God, it orients our hearts so that when God wants to move, we can be receptive to that movement.

THE PRACTICE OF STILLNESS AS A SPIRITUAL DISCIPLINE
PROVIDES A GROUNDED LANDSCAPE FOR REFLECTION
AND HONEST APPRAISAL.

As mentioned earlier, things look different within and after a moment of profound graced stillness. A new clarity can emerge. There is an unclutteredness about the experience that reveals many of our worries and preoccupations as superficial. In this place of stillness, our souls can anchor themselves. They can ground themselves in a stable and trustworthy space.

From a still point, a space for reflection becomes possible. This reflection is not the type which requires excessive deliberation and energy. This reflection is infused with divine light and presence. A transcendent presence to ourselves through God can shed new light on questions and concerns in our everyday life. Within that heightened awareness, an "appraisal" can take place. We appraise or look again reflectively in the light of the Spirit at our situations, our choices, our behaviors. Our relations with others take on a new hue in the light of transcendent awareness. God's perspective colors the way we look at our approach to life. The need for charity, compassion, or patience is revealed and from that appraisal decisions for change emerge.

This appraisal is honest. We no longer want to deceive ourselves with the cloudy perceptions of our own minds. Rather, in the moment of awareness of God, we let down our defenses and let God's love melt away our resistance. We put down the shield which we may have used to distance ourselves from truth about our mixed motives or anxieties. God's love brings us to a more transparent honesty about our foibles and misdemeanors without fear of judgment. From this place of transcendent self-presence, we can review our life and make alterations that are more in line with the Divine One. We can examine our consciousness and revise it, realigning it with that sacred mystery.

In stillness, a reappraisal of our way of thinking can occur easily because we are illuminated by the light of God. That light is one of love, acceptance, and truth. Stillness facilitates the possibility of ongoing mini-conversions on a daily basis.

These are merely four of many benefits the practice of stillness introduces to our spiritual life. But how does one go about practicing stillness as a spiritual discipline in everyday life? Isn't this a practice that is too lofty for those of us with busy lives? Or are there concrete environments and activities that can foster stillness?

The Practice of Stillness as a Spiritual Discipline

The practice of stillness is obviously most readily facilitated in environments of silence. There are great souls who can meditate and move into profound stillness in the middle of a busy airport terminal, but most of us can't. Here it is important to know which places naturally predispose us to a quieter frame of mind. Although these will, to some degree, be unique to each of us, they may have certain things in common.

Many people find that natural environments are the most immediately helpful in the practice of stillness. Places of organic wonder and awe are not hard to name. When asked to name them, people will often spontaneously respond with answers like "Oh, the ocean," or "the mountains," or "a secluded lake." There is something about these places of nature that automatically drops us into stillness. Because of our past experiences in such places, we are already predisposed to stillness there.

In the first part of this book I mentioned a number of places that could be conducive to an encounter with God in stillness. Whether it is under the night sky, before the lit tabernacle candle in the sanctuary of a church, or in the privacy of a special hidden place that has meaning for us, we enter into a hushed expectancy. These places foundationally help us gear down inside so that we can move into deeper attentiveness.

In addition to certain places, some activities can lead us into greater stillness. Some years ago I discovered that I love the quiet stillness of swimming underwater. My senses are shut off from the normal noise above water and there is something primordial in the floating experience beneath the surface. It's like being in a womb, suspended in the amniotic fluid of the earth, calm and open.

The rhythm of a simple routine in life can foster stillness, too, especially when it is accompanied by solitude and we have time to relax with it. When I have time to iron contemplatively, I love doing it. The practice of easing out those wrinkles in a focused, quiet way can slow me down and facilitate my entering into stillness.

Here we come to an important point. Stillness is directly connected with the discipline of slowing down. As we have already noted, slowing down is one of the foundational practices for developing contemplative consciousness and supporting the other disciplines discussed in this book. The interior simplification resulting from slowing down facilitates a more ready descent into stillness.

Stillness and slowing down take time. Too often we find ourselves expecting to experience stillness immediately when we begin the practice. We are disappointed when we can't enter easily into a quiet, focused interiority. But our expectation may be unrealistic. I remember once being chided by a spiritual director for my attempts to drop down into stillness within five minutes after I started to pray. She reminded me that if my interest was to foster a more contemplative way of being, I must also adapt my lifestyle a bit. "You can't just drop into stillness immediately when you've been flying around all day," she said to me. The rhythms and pace in the rest of life need to be altered so that they reflect a contemplative desire. It takes time to enter into depth.

The phrase she used, "flying around all day," made me think of a metaphor—the Concorde jetliner. What would happen if a pilot attempted to land a Concorde on a dime? This airplane goes faster than the speed of sound in transatlantic flight. That kind of speed requires extra time to prepare for landing and extra space to land. To suddenly bring down the plane and stop it on a short runway would cause massive damage to the aircraft and its instruments. It is not built to come to an immediate stop.

How many of us are charging around like little Concordes? Slowing down and entering into stillness require a more gradual shift for us, as well. We must take into account how organically we might need a little extra time to make the transition into quiet.

Sue Monk Kidd's wisdom is pertinent here:

> We need to find the point in our soul where we go neither forward nor backward but are fastened in our waiting.... Our minds can become clogged with the busyness and details of living—things that make us fret and squirm, things that make us run from the waiting and the slow greening of our soul. That's when we need to pause and reconnect ourselves to the still point.[2]

Let us now look at the practice of pausing.

A Concrete Practice of Stillness: Pausing

A concrete experience of stillness is that of "pausing." When we pause, we imprint again the felt experience of stillness. Within moments of pausing, we can remind ourselves of that bigger picture for which we hunger. We stop and take a breath with a certain mindfulness. We shift our attention briefly to the God whom we seek.

There are a number of ways of practicing "pausing." There are "natural" pauses in our day that can allow for a momentary refocusing. Such pauses are those at the end of the day, when we tuck our children in, when we sit down briefly in the quiet of evening. There are also the missed pauses in the bathroom, when we have to take a moment to do our business anyway. The power of bathroom pauses to reconnect us with stillness is often overlooked. An entire book could be written on "bathroom spirituality" and opportunities we could avail ourselves of in our private times.

Then there are "intentional" pauses. These are pauses we structure in to help us focus on God. They may be moments of meditation to which we deliberately give ourselves. There is the pause (often omitted) after the reception of communion. My father used to "make a visit" and stop into the church on his way home from work. In these moments, we intentionally remind ourselves of our focus and desire for stillness. They may be brief, but they can help shape our awareness of God.

Finally, there are "surprise" pauses. These are the moments when we get "caught up" by a gift from God. We may be awed by a sunset, its colors and its expanse. It is so lovely that we stop in our movement and drink it in. We may be confronted with a traffic jam and have to make a decision about the style of waiting that we want to practice. We may choose to pause at the wonder of the first crocus, flowering beside the sidewalk. We can take a deep breath and momentarily reconnect with the Creator of that beauty at our feet.

It is in the simple activity of our day that our awareness of God can reawaken. In the pauses of life, we can consciously become aware that we have before us moments of stillness through which we can "log-on" with God. These help orient us toward longer periods of time for stillness in retreat, vacation, or prayer when we are able to give ourselves to these. In the meantime, we can "touch base" with God to keep ourselves attuned to the mystery.

Questions for Our Practice of Stillness

With these reflections in mind, let us ponder a few questions with regard to our practice of stillness. If we take some time to consider our own responses to these, we may identify how stillness is already hidden within our day.

Where can you give yourself to pauses for stillness in your everyday life?

What places move you to stillness?

Can you get to those places more often?

When were you last "captured by stillness"? Has it been a while? Why?

What helps you to become still inside and remain there?

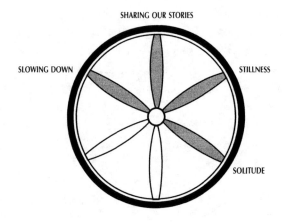

SHARING OUR STORIES

SLOWING DOWN

STILLNESS

SOLITUDE

SOLITUDE

Early Sunday morning I was packing a suitcase, preparing to leave my home to direct an eight-day retreat at a retreat house ninety miles away. I was grouchy about the long drive and leaving my comfortable little house and my husband for a week, and I was antsy about all the projects that would be put on hold during my absence. Like a tired infant who fusses against the need for sleep, I was fighting in my interior against the discomfort of moving from an active, overstimulated life to a space of silence, listening, and aloneness. In my head, I knew this solitude would do me good and was long overdue, but my body resisted the quieting down and the asceticism of leaving the familiar busyness behind to enter into a place of simply being.

An hour and a half later, I arrived at the retreat house. Having driven alone in my car, I had had the opportunity to gear down inside. I had begun to breathe and connect with deeper hungers within me.

After depositing my luggage in my room, I walked down to the chapel. The ambiance of this sacred space enveloped me. I sank down into the pillow on the floor and drank deeply of the silence. "Oh my God," I exclaimed, "I forgot how good this feels."

The fifth spiritual practice is solitude. Coupled with stillness, solitude is essential for anchoring us in our innermost beings. Solitude can not only reinforce and support our integrity, it can protect our individual health and the sanity of society.

Thomas Merton spoke of the linkage between the unique solitude of persons and the general health of society in his book *Thoughts in Solitude:*

In actual fact, society depends for its existence on the inviolable personal solitude of its members. ...To be a person implies responsibility and freedom, and both of these imply a certain interior solitude, a sense of personal integrity, a sense of one's own reality and of one's ability to give himself to society—or to refuse that gift.[1]

Merton sees the connection between the integrity of the society and the integrity of each of its members. Solitude is the spiritual practice that allows each of us to reflect on our own reality and then determine how we will contribute to the stability of the whole.

The Spiritual Benefits of Solitude

In contrast to the other five "s" words, solitude has long been identified as a spiritual practice. Each major world tradition has literature that instructs individuals on embracing solitude and allowing it to deepen their spiritual lives. Let us look at three ways in which the practice of solitude contributes to deepening our spiritual lives.

THE PRACTICE OF SOLITUDE NURTURES OUR INTIMACY WITH GOD AND OURSELVES.

As stated in our definition of spirituality, whenever we foster intimacy with God we are aiding the spiritual dimension of our lives. Solitude naturally allows us to get in touch with ourselves, but it also promotes our connection with the sacred. It provides an opportunity to "come home" to our foundational selves. It allows us to get underneath the facades that we sometimes create to survive in this world, to rest in the truth of who we know ourselves most deeply to be.

In solitude, we have a period of time in which to view ourselves unmasked, complete with blemishes and beauty. We familiarize ourselves again with the uniqueness of our own personhood. Solitude allows us to revel in the parts of ourselves we need to celebrate and to begin to repair the parts that otherwise could go unnoticed.

IN SOLITUDE, WE GIVE OURSELVES TIME TO SIFT THROUGH AND FILTER OUR CHOICES.

Solitude provides an opportunity to live reflectively. In our depths, we can begin to look calmly at our behaviors and choices. We can reflect on their life-giving aspects. Are our behaviors and choices consonant with who we want to be? Are they harmonious with who we say we want to become? We have the time in our practice of solitude to sift through the movements, attitudes, and feelings that come up in our busy lives. We can also check our motivations for what we do.

When we become aware of the interior movements and the external behaviors that come forth from our choices, we can sort through all the bits of information to assess their appropriateness for us. Our personal integrity, the healthy integration of life events into our true selves, is dependent on our honest appraisal of our behaviors and choices. Solitude allows us to identify those things that are opposed to our welfare. Our practice of solitude helps us catch deformative habits and patterns before they become solidified into dispositions out of which we regularly act. It challenges an unreflective mode of being and supplants it with awakened, aware self-groundedness. Thus, we can choose proactively with knowledge rather than reactively without reflection.

THE PRACTICE OF SOLITUDE OFFERS US
AN INTERIOR PLACE FOR INTEGRATION.

Many stimuli come at us in one day. The glut of possibilities, information, and options in the modern world is staggering. Sometimes we feel assaulted by the amount of stress we are asked to deal with emotionally, physically, and spiritually. The cumulative effects of all the input from the media, our churches and schools, and our family life can become overwhelming unless we foster a spiritual centering through solitude.

The practice of solitude offers us a space in our day in which we can distance ourselves from the glut, breathe, and integrate our experience. In the privacy of our own souls, we can resonate in a deeper freedom. Solitude provides a time for absorption of that which is generative for us. A reverence for our own selves as persons can emerge and lead us to a gentler way of being in the world. The breathing space of solitude gives us the perspective to see the events of life and the opportunity to name the different voices that beckon to us. The practice of solitude helps us to discern that which is truly formative for us. We can integrate that which is helpful to our spiritual vitality and let go of that which is unnecessary.

Solitude has many other benefits, and we could find extensive lists of these in the writings of spiritual authors. For now, however, let us move on to the actual practice of solitude and how to foster it in our daily lives.

The Practice of Solitude

How do we begin the practice of solitude as a spiritual discipline? The practice of solitude, like the practice of stillness, is most readily facilitated in silent environments. It is also most enhanced by situations of aloneness.

It is important to note that when we speak of the spiritual practice of solitude, we are speaking of a formative aloneness that is not to be confused with isolation. Isolation can cause a contraction of the person, internally and externally. It can pull the person inward, away from others and away from the sacred connection with the larger mystery of God. It is often a defensive move that is the result of being shamed or humiliated. A person who feels overwhelmed by the demands of survival may retreat into isolation for self-preservation. If this becomes a regular mode of behavior, it can turn tragic. A social and emotional erosion can occur which can lead to depression, pathology, and even suicide.

Formative solitude counteracts this defensive reaction by providing a space for safe integration and interior connection. Within formative solitude, aloneness is no longer an escape. Rather, aloneness becomes a way to embrace the solitariness of our existence, the uniqueness of our persons, and the individuality that is our unique contribution to the world.

From a spiritual viewpoint, solitude allows us to reconnect with something bigger than ourselves through which we discover our being. Carolyn Gratton states:

> Human hearts come to the knowledge of their treasure not by focusing their consciousness on what can be rationally understood or logically communicated, but by being silent and receptive to the touch of an invisible presence.[2]

We come to know our own significance and worth within moments of formative solitude and prayer. We hear our own voice responded to by the whisper of God. In solitude we become familiar with God's voice, and we gradually become more skilled at distinguishing it from the multiplicity of other voices that can distract us.

For the practice of solitude, environments of silence and situations of aloneness can be helpful to us. In addition to those mentioned previously, there are other environments and situations that can be conducive to solitude. A friend and I used to speak of our fondness for cemeteries. Where else in today's world can one experience the kind of silence and aloneness to be found in a well-groomed cemetery? People have also spoken of their love for the city in the early hours of the morning. Many urban dwellers find in the silence and the solitude of being the only one awake an environment conducive to the practice of solitude. There is also something about places of immensity which can renew the sense of solitude and place within a larger sphere. The desert or prairie can be a place of great nourishment for those who have become comfortable with being alone with themselves, without the frills of consumer society.

A sense of ease in being alone with ourselves can take time. To become comfortable in solitude we must recognize the need for compassion with ourselves and our own adjustment process to aloneness. On a retreat, I often find that it takes me a full four days before I am ready for and open to deep solitude. Making the transition to that inner landscape can be initially difficult. The transition to solitude is as problematic as the move to stillness.

Two wise insights from the contemplative tradition may be helpful here. First of all, it is important to accept the fact that ambiguity is an essential part of the spiritual life. Often what we find most uncomfortable is entering into a place where we do not have all the answers. The "not knowing" is hard for us. In the spiritual life, as in the rest of life, we will never have it all figured out. We will never be totally in control. What solitude allows us to do is to enter into the grayness and ambiguity more graciously and to remain poised and relatively at ease within the "not knowing" in our own interiors.

Second, it is helpful to remember as we enter into aloneness that loneliness is also part of the spiritual life. As we move deeply into the depths of intimacy with ourselves and our God, there will be lonely patches. It is, to a certain degree, a solitary venture. Merton confirms this, saying that a person

> becomes a solitary at the moment when, no matter what may be his external surroundings, he is suddenly aware of his own inalienable solitude and sees that he will never be anything but solitary. From that moment, solitude is not potential—it is actual.[3]

Previous generations seemed to accept the reality of loneliness with less of a struggle. My grandparents appeared to assume that loneliness was simply an unavoidable part of life. There would naturally be periods of time when loneliness occurred. Today, it seems many of us assume that something is wrong when we experience some loneliness. Our consumer society conditions us to expect that we should somehow be able to fix this. A cure might involve a job change, a relational shift, a new car, or sexual gratification. There is a mad dash to fill up the loneliness with something that will make it feel less uncomfortable.

The practice of solitude invites us to become more adept at entering into aloneness and allowing its formative impact to affect us. By relaxing in the loneliness and accepting it as a permissible reality, we cease struggling with it and instead learn to ride it like a surfer rides a wave. We are not toppled by it. It becomes less threatening and less ominous.

In a deliberate practice of solitude we stretch our capacity to live with both ambiguity and loneliness. To do this, we must develop "postures of the heart" that enable us to become aware of what God is doing in us in alone time.[4] These interior postures can gradually bring us more wholeheartedly to say "yes" to all that God wants for us.

Questions for Our Practice of Solitude

In slowing down, sharing our stories, giving ourselves to stillness and solitude, we prepare ourselves well for the fifth and sixth spiritual disciplines of surrender and solidarity. To a certain degree, we have a responsibility to self and society to maintain some solitude. Out of respect for the integrity of ourselves and our community, we must give ourselves to some interior time. Again we hear Thomas Merton remind us that "the truest solitude is not something outside [us], not an absence of men or of sound around [us]; it is an abyss opening up in the center of [our] own soul."[5]

Solitude is the grounding time that allows us to become comfortable with that abyss. It is an incarnate opportunity to sort through the plethora of directives from other people, the world, and our own interiors to discern the voice of God. That voice is not foreign to us. Deep down inside, we know the voice we want to hear. It is a familiar voice, a voice we have heard before, even as far back as childhood, but we need to be properly disposed to hear it. In solitude we go into silence to listen and to resonate with God's affirmation and challenge to us.

Some questions may be helpful for us as we reflect on our own practice of solitude. We might find that in order to respond to these questions wholeheartedly and honestly, we actually have to practice some solitude and go apart for a while. This action in itself testifies to our earnest desire to give ourselves to the practice. As we enter into solitude, truth will reveal itself more readily within the answers we generate.

Can you "be" alone with yourself?

What helps you avoid the temptation to run back to noise and busyness, missing out on the riches of being alone for a while?

What facilitates formative solitude for you? What environments of silence? What situations of aloneness?

When did you last hear that "voice" that you know and hunger for? Can you remember the circumstances around it and what led up to it?

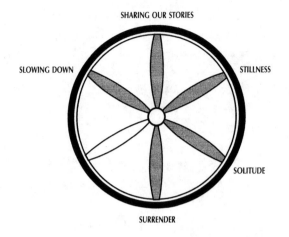

SHARING OUR STORIES

SLOWING DOWN

STILLNESS

SOLITUDE

SURRENDER

SURRENDER

"Caleb, you have to let go or you're dead."

Caleb shivered in his swimsuit as he balanced on the L-shaped branch that jutted out over the edge of the swollen lake. He was clutching the knotted end of a rope that was attached to the stout branch above him. He could see that letting go would be crucial here. If he swung out hanging onto the rope and refused to surrender his grip, he would snap back against the tree and mash his bare skin against the bark.

His father yelled to him again, "You've got to let go." His nine-year-old pal, Joshua, urged him on by modeling a perfect splash as he flung himself into the water.

Caleb faces the same stress we each struggle with in our efforts to surrender. We want to hang onto what we know is safe. We will not know what is underneath the water until we risk letting go. When we summon up the courage, we are often rewarded with a delight and freedom that we may not have anticipated. But first we must take a chance.

Just like Caleb, each of us has the opportunity to practice the spiritual discipline of surrender every day in ordinary situations. We are surrounded by a panoply of possibilities to let go and let surrender work for us in developing greater flexibility and freedom in our interior life.

In Caleb's case, surrender is not simply a discipline of the spirit. He knows in his flesh what refusing to surrender feels like. It feels like tight muscles, a tense jaw, a wobbly stomach. It is an uncomfortable and tense state. But as he takes up the challenge and swings out over the lake, he lets go and slips into the smooth waters. An ecstatic shriek resounds when he surfaces. He is elated with his triumph, thrilled with the sensations, and relieved of all his fear. He knows now the corresponding jubilation that letting go offers.

Surrender is perhaps the most difficult of the six spiritual disciplines outlined in this book. Fundamentally, it goes against the human propensity to take control. Caleb surrenders his control and leaps into literal darkness in his letting go. Most of us experience some risk in the face of every surrender. Surrender requires us to let go, to loosen the grip that our need to control has on us. How is surrender a "spiritual" discipline?

The Spiritual Benefits of Surrender

Surrender is pivotal for the spiritual life. An orientation toward surrender is as foundational a discipline as slowing down. This is where transformative intimacy with God can

occur. Christian spirituality is grounded in the ability to walk
in the way of Christ as a person surrendered to God. Letting
go is fundamental to the spiritual life. As in Gethsemane, it
is often in the midst of ambiguity and confusion that we
must surrender to mystery so that our faith life may be refined. We must detach from familiar ways in order to leap
out into the unknown. Surrender is a letting go that, while it
holds much potential for freedom, also requires freedom.

In looking at the discipline of surrender as a spiritual
practice, let us begin by exploring four elements that are
part of "letting go."

THE PRACTICE OF SURRENDER IS A FORM OF DETACHMENT.

A major obstacle to spiritual depth is attachment. Classical spiritual literature instructs us on the dangers of attachment, reminding us that inordinate desires thwart our movement on the spiritual path. Surrender is a remedy to that
obsessive tendency of which we may not even be aware. "We
cannot see things in perspective until we cease to hug them
to our own bosom," writes Thomas Merton. "When we let
go of them we begin to appreciate them as they really are.
Only then can we begin to see God in them."[1]

Attachment holds us and the other captive. Whether
our attachment is to an image of God, another person, or
our own notion of how things should be done, if that attachment is inordinate, we hold the other imprisoned
within a projection of what we want it to be. We miss seeing
reality as it truly is. When we begin to surrender, we loosen
our grip on the other and allow it to assume its true dimensions. We let it have its own autonomy. We free ourselves,
too, from a narrow perception which may be constricting
us. Detachment allows both the other and ourselves to

bloom more readily and freely. Detachment always involves surrender.

TO PRACTICE SURRENDER WE MUST FEEL SAFE.

Letting go requires a sense of safety. Few of us could readily let go of something we valued unless we felt it was safe to do so. External safety is very significant in providing the fundamental security needed to truly let go. If we feel the world is safe, we can more naturally relax into a trusting stance.

However, internal safety is even more important. A sense of internal safety stems from a fundamental gift of stability given to us by parents, family, and church. But even if this was flawed, we can develop a sense of internal safety by cultivating a solid faith relationship with God. Storing up a rich treasure chest of memories from prayer, worship, human encounters, and spiritual reading can provide us with a foundation full of confidence in the divine. Feeling blessed with abundance, we can let go of lesser attachments that impede our spiritual freedom.

Detachment happens more readily when we view ourselves as fundamentally rich. If we are in a position of security, we can let go gently. "Real self-conquest is the conquest of ourselves, not by ourselves, but by the Holy Spirit. Self-conquest is really self-surrender. Yet, before we can surrender ourselves, we must become ourselves, for no one can give up what he does not possess."[2] Fundamental security is essential for letting go.

A sense of internal safety will allow us to surrender, even under extreme circumstances, in an action that could confound human comprehension. It was a foundational safety in relation to God and self that allowed a person like Maximilian Kolbe to surrender his life into the hands of Nazis for the sake of a bigger purpose. Kolbe stepped forward and offered his own life as a substitute for another who was to be killed. His external environment was far from safe, but his internal knowledge of himself and his intimacy with God provided the confidence that it was safe to do such a radical thing. He was profoundly secure in his sense of God. This surrender would not guarantee protection from illness or death. But a phenomenal freedom accompanied his faithfulness and provided him with a larger capacity to give of himself. Maximilian Kolbe lost his life, but gained it back in the image of Jesus Christ himself.

THE PRACTICE OF SURRENDER REQUIRES READINESS.

Organically, surrender comes more fluidly when we are ready. Whether in transition or in a time of stability, we need time to adjust, heal, let go, and be transformed. Surrender should not be forced. It can require waiting and patience. If we try to push ourselves into surrender in an act of righteous willfulness, we perpetuate the same violence that our attachment is causing us. An attempt to gain control by forcing ourselves into submission is an abuse of power used against ourselves.

True surrender is not a willful imposition, however well meaning. It is marked, rather, by the signs of the Spirit, such as love, joy, peace, patience, kindness, goodness, faithfulness, gentleness, and self-control. Our bodies, minds, and hearts grow into readiness in their own time. God respects the stages of that process. If surrender is to be formative, the heart must soften tenderly into it.

The interesting reality is that many people who pray earnestly for the grace to surrender, knowing that it is beyond their power, may find one day that they awaken with a naturally surrendered heart. The clinging has stopped. They may have affirmed the process by deliberately choosing to move toward surrender, but the actual power to surrender occurred through God's initiative and grace. It is almost as if, while they slept, their hearts were made tender and ready by the Holy Spirit for the letting go. It is a process much like forgiveness; when we are really primed, the gift is bestowed upon us and our internal selves are freed. There is great rejoicing among those who humbly and consciously become aware that such a gift has been given. When we let go in concert with the Spirit, the healing is thorough and complete.

SURRENDER REQUIRES THE DEVELOPMENT AND APPLICATION
OF THE DISPOSITIONS OF GENTLENESS AND FIRMNESS.

To surrender gracefully, the two dispositions of gentleness and firmness should be held in balance. Excessive gentleness can result in a wishy-washy indecisiveness, whereas firmness without the check of gentleness can become tyranny. When we practice surrender, both of these interior orientations must be respected and developed in an integrated approach to ourselves. Firmness, informed by gentleness, will allow us to identify the places where there is a need for change and follow through with a heart that is, while steadfast, not judgmental or self-critical. Gentleness will give us time to breathe in and absorb the significance of the ascetical call to surrender as we move to acting on it.

The development and application of gentleness may come more easily when it is directed at another person. It is sometimes far more difficult for us to apply it to ourselves. We are not accustomed to approaching ourselves with tenderness. Our tendency may be to "stay tough" in dealing with difficult life events or changes. We need to cultivate a sensitivity toward our own rhythm and timing in letting go, a sensitivity like that which we would offer another person in a similar situation. When practiced consciously, the cultivation of sensitivity toward ourselves has the benefit of affecting our compassion for others.

The practice of surrender involves a fundamental stretching of our capacity to say "Yes." It involves taking up everyday opportunities to turn the control in our lives over to the bigger mystery of God and trust that "all will be well."[3] It involves admitting that what we cling to is a substitute for full commitment to God. Surrender asks us to pry our fingers off those surrogate divinities and open ourselves to a life under the direction of the Spirit.

The Practice of Surrender

How do we begin to practice surrender as a spiritual discipline? Many of us overlook events within our daily life that already afford us an opportunity to consciously practice the spiritual discipline of surrender. We can start our practice of surrender by raising our awareness of where the possibilities for its implementation are within daily life.

Some years ago, I was directing a sabbatical program for priests and religious from all over the world. My employer and I were both very attentive to extending generous hospitality to all of our guests, especially those coming from overseas. We were expecting the arrival of one person from the Far East, but had been given no information as to his arrival time, his flight, or his plans for transport to the sabbatical site. I was in a great quandary. How could I do my job well and graciously welcome him without this information? The two of us made phone calls, sent faxes, and attempted to contact appropriate authorities to make sure that he would not be left stranded at the airport. All of our efforts were to no avail. There was no way of contacting him and making appropriate arrangements for him.

Finally, I turned to my employer with some anxiety and frustration. "So, what do we do?" I asked. His response continues to guide my awareness to this day. He simply said, "Well, Nicki, it looks like this is an opportunity to practice surrender." I was startled. I would never have made the connection between this real-life dilemma and the practice of a spiritual discipline. I took a deep breath and let go. Eventually, the man arrived safely without our intervention and I learned more about the value of letting go in my practice of surrender.

The first step in practicing surrender, then, is awareness: being aware that an opportunity is before us through which we can trust God's providence and, by using mundane events, grow in our spiritual life. Our mindfulness of these invitations increases our ease with abandoning ourselves to the divine, even in the minutiae of everyday life.

A second help in developing our practice of surrender is identifying the attachments we have that require surrender. There are two types of detachment that involve an abandonment of self:

(1) an active type of detachment, which involves taking proactive steps to deal with those attachments of which we are conscious, and

(2) a deeper type of detachment which, because it has to do with "secret attachments," we must acknowledge requires the initiative of God.[4]

The active type of detachment begins with our identifying the areas of our lives where attachment is blocking our
fullest response to and freedom before God. These are the
places where we can intentionally apply ourselves to reform.
Our religious tradition may offer instruction which can
guide our efforts. We can devise deliberate methods to help
ourselves change the habits that are impeding us. This may
involve curbing desires, addressing distractions, or curtailing
activities that we know inhibit our spiritual maturation.
Areas needing change may include physical, social, relational, and spiritual patterns that are counter to charity,
mercy, wisdom, and health.

During Advent some years ago, when my husband and I
were first married, we decided that it would be helpful to us
spiritually to consciously reform some problematic habits.
We had both become aware that we had grown lax in our use
of certain cultural slang words in our speech. We resolved to
do something about this. To remind ourselves, we posted on
the refrigerator an 8" x 10" notice that said, "Stop swearing,
dammit!" Then we placed an empty mason jar on the top of
the refrigerator and put in a quarter for each infraction of
our Advent resolution. This money was to go to the missions
as a Christmas present. One result was that the missions did
quite well that year. The other result was closer to home.
Our habit had definitely needed reform and the Advent project raised our awareness of how ingrained it had become in
our everyday speech. On an active level, we weaned ourselves from laziness in our vocabulary and altered the pattern
with deliberate attentiveness.

On a deeper level, surrender in self-abandonment can
happen on the "secret attachments," which are beyond our
control. While we may be aware that they block our full
spiritual vitality, the effort needed to move beyond them is

bigger than that which we can orchestrate. Detachment from these "secret attachments" must be left to the initiative of God. The night must empty us of our clinging to them.

Detachment from such attachments—whether to an image of God, an addiction, or a willful way of being—is grace-dependent. It cannot be accomplished by an act of the will. Our will is involved in consenting to the surrendering process, but the ultimate purification and integration are very much in the hands of God.

In essence, our *willfulness* must be gently transformed into *willingness*. The approach we take to surrender must be one of openness, readiness, and willingness without a forceful assertion of our own preferences. Most occasions of surrender require us to evaluate our underlying need for control. They are opportunities for us to open ourselves up for change which is difficult for us. What we are really learning to surrender in these moments is the self. Our being is undergoing a conversion process that will allow us to conquer our selfish tendencies and move into greater self-surrender.

How do we handle the difficult process of detachment? The development of three attitudes can ease the tension. We already know that the development of tenderness toward ourselves balanced with firmness is essential. Added to this is the development of a fundamental receptivity to all of God's surprises. This receptivity is the basis for a more contemplative openness and tranquillity which can help us move through the difficult transitions in our detachment process.

Finally, developing a willingness to weep can be extremely helpful. Detachment is often painful. It sometimes hurts to let go. For healing to taking place, it is necessary that we acknowledge that surrender is costing us something, and then give ourselves permission to weep over the loss. A willingness to weep is an acknowledgment that we are fallible, feeling creatures who need to express our suffering in bodily ways. Kept inside, this pain can make us bitter. Released in tears, the emotional pain no longer holds us captive. Tears clear the way for greater freedom and health.

Sometimes we know we need to surrender, but we just can't do it. Even our desire for surrender remains only a remote possibility. There are many miles our soul has to travel to even be willing to let go. In these cases, we must begin the movement toward surrender by praying for the grace to merely desire surrender.[5] The gradual orientation of our minds, our hearts, and our wills toward letting go may take considerable time. God honors that process, the organic rhythm of readiness that brings us to the point at which our earnest hearts humbly admit their limitations. The Holy Spirit can work in a heart that, even in resistance, desires to desire the good. Like a butterfly in a cocoon, the beauty that is gestating in the quiet will eventually bloom into a new wholeness.

Disposing ourselves to a surrendered life means consciously affirming the practice of letting go each day. My father used to have a "Morning Offering" prayer card pasted on the mirror of his bathroom. As an adolescent, I thought this was somewhat pious and hokey. Now that I am an adult, I realize that, as he shaved, my father could refer to the card as the first prayer of his day. This prayer oriented him toward living a surrendered life in relation to God. "O my God, I offer you my prayers, works, joys and sufferings of this day..." The placement of that prayer on his mirror fastened his mind to a right relationship with God for this short span of his life.

For us, it may be helpful to identify little acts of surrender that we could weave into our day. These gestures may be very quiet and unobtrusive. They may not even be identifiable as "holy acts" by others looking on. But the conscious practice of these little acts of surrender within daily life prepares us for the larger surrenders that will be asked of us. The way we negotiate small acts of letting go will assist us in negotiating more significant surrenders in ill health, aging, separation, loss, and ultimately death.

Each little act of surrender helps us orient ourselves toward a surrendered way of being. With gentleness and firmness we can consciously turn our souls toward God like a sail in the wind, catching the full benefit of the gust. Each moment can become a moment full of potential, filled up with the breath of the Holy Spirit. Gradually, as we steer our course along the way, the practice of surrender becomes embedded in our way of being. In synchrony with the Spirit, we simplify, let go, and sail smoothly under the direction of the Holy.

Questions for Our Practice of Surrender

Surrender occurs most easily when we have been predisposed to it by the practices of slowing down, sharing our stories, stillness, and solitude. As we grow accustomed to the practice of each of these, we become less hard-edged and more tender in our attitudes toward ourselves and life. This "tenderizing" allows us to let go without clinging. It allows us to surrender the control that sometimes holds us spiritually captive.

Some questions might assist us in looking at our present practice of surrender, as well as preparing us for other forms of letting go. Hidden within the reality of our present lives lie opportunities for spiritual freedom and maturity. As we practice surrender in the everyday, the tightness of holding onto our own agendas, anxieties, or anticipations is loosened into an open, willing stance toward life and toward God. Our bodies and our souls benefit from a healthier, freer way of being that releases us from a subtly belligerent insistence that things must go our way. Instead, we can learn to laugh more readily and trust a God who wants everything good for us.

> *How open are you to letting go? How ready are you?*

> *Where do you most relax and feel safe with God?*

> *Where did you feel the call to surrender yesterday? How did you respond to it?*

> *What little gesture of surrender would remind you daily of your dependence on God?*

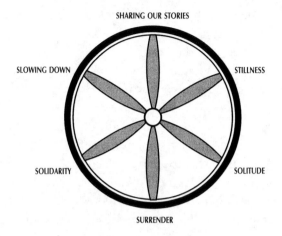

SHARING OUR STORIES

SLOWING DOWN

STILLNESS

SOLIDARITY

SOLITUDE

SURRENDER

SOLIDARITY

Wearing heels and a dress suit, she stood between the first and second marble steps leading up to the altar. The instruction had been that all the graduates, celebrating their completion of Divinity School, would circle the altar for a blessing. Lack of awareness had led to an oversight which resulted in one class member with a disability remaining at the foot of the steps, unable to get up to the altar.

The class had assembled and begged Chris to complete their circle by joining them at the altar. She refused. Rather, like a bridge extending between her colleague in a wheelchair at the foot of the steps and the circle of graduates gathered around the altar, she stood gracefully challenging the lack of accessibility. She would not exclude anyone.

It came naturally to her, this act of solidarity, she said later. Having cared for a disabled husband, she readily moved into the position of one who reached out to include and connect. She stood easily in this middle place so that no one would be left out.

Solidarity has not been traditionally seen as a "spiritual" discipline. Yet, the other five practices could describe a relatively limited, interior spirituality; without this sixth spiritual practice, the wheel is incomplete. The practice of solidarity pulls the other disciplines—those of slowing down, sharing our stories, stillness, solitude, and surrender—into the social context. It is the spiritual discipline that responsibly links us with the larger creation and a broader human community. More necessary than ever in our historical evolution, it is the practice that binds us to one another and invites us to move beyond the narrow perimeters of our own perception to unite with others. It is the extension of our souls to embrace others and acknowledge our relationship with the planet.

Solidarity flows naturally from the practice of the other five disciplines. After we have slowed down, shared our stories, stepped back into stillness and solitude, then moved into surrender, we are ripe for an outward movement that connects us with others. The outflowing of genuine surrender allows us to fall into "right relationship" with God and with all of God's creation. A deeper harmony and sense of at-oneness can emerge. This form of intimacy in relationship with the world generates greater responsiveness.

We get some intimation of what solidarity means when we share our stories. A sense of connectedness may be glimpsed as people interpersonally invest in one another and find an affinity in that sharing. But this connection needs to radiate out beyond the immediacy of proximate interpersonal sharing into acts of responsible, sensible stewardship and social care. Rooted in our sense of the divine and our surrender in right relationship to God, the practice of solidarity "disposes us to a generous yet congenial availability to others and to the work of justice, peace, and mercy in this world."[1]

The Spiritual Benefits of Solidarity

What are the benefits of the organic spiritual discipline of solidarity? Let us examine three specific benefits that contribute to our spiritual growth in depth and maturity.

THE PRACTICE OF SOLIDARITY FOSTERS HUMILITY IN RIGHT RELATIONSHIP WITH GOD.

As mentioned earlier, the experience of humility in our spiritual life is always a help to our spiritual growth. When we practice solidarity, we heighten our awareness that we live in dependency on God, who is creator and sustainer of our existence. In our awareness of God's beneficence, we become conscious of God's generosity. The seamless coordination of all creation in sustaining and generating life is awe-inspiring. A sense of wonder is naturally evoked as we reflect on the genius behind it all.

When we are in touch with the generosity of the Creator, we are more likely to get in touch with our own creatureliness. Creatureliness may not be a fashionable term in an era of human mastery. Yet, our "right relationship" with God demands a healthy, humble admission that we are neither the originators of our existence nor the engineers of our own evolution. The Master Builder has given us limited ability to co-create. Our proper response to that awareness is humble assent and attentive listening to the directives of the divine for ongoing nurturance and creativity.

When we begin to practice solidarity on a local, regional, or global level, we participate to some degree in the unfolding of the universe. We accept our role as co-creators and develop wise stewardship processes that foster and contribute to the sustenance of our world and its people. "Created in the image and likeness" of the One who created all of us, we humbly offer our talents in contributing to the life-promoting agenda of the mystery of formation.

THE PRACTICE OF SOLIDARITY GENERATES AFFINITY
IN RIGHT RELATIONSHIP WITH OTHERS.

A sense of humility in right relationship with God will affect the way we relate with others created by God. A respectful approach to those whom God has created is an extension of appropriate reverence for God. When we begin consciously to see ourselves in equal relationship with other creatures, a sense of affinity and humility is fostered.

It is all too easy in our day to distance ourselves from a fundamental sense of relationship with the other persons who share the earth. At times our relational sensitivity is blunted by the demands of culture, work, and survival. We may find our hearts overwhelmed and feel we want to distance ourselves from the acute need we see depicted on television and in the print media.

The practice of solidarity invites us to reconsider retreating from concern. When anchored in the balanced practice of the other five disciplines, it can reawaken in us a sense of affinity and connectedness with other human beings. This affinity heals the alienation that can develop when we are rushed, driven, or overwhelmed. The practice of solidarity allows for a felt experience of bonding to remind us of a larger relationship and stimulate a heartfelt generosity in response to other people's needs.

THE PRACTICE OF SOLIDARITY AS A SPIRITUAL DISCIPLINE
BROADENS OUR SENSE OF RELATIONALITY.

Right relationship with God and with other human beings leads to right relationship with God's creation. When we truly take on the mind of the Creator, we begin to view all of creation through a compassionate and loving lens. Our relationship with the planet, each other, and ourselves begins to change. We are a part of the whole, intimately interconnected with other beings. Solidarity broadens our sense of relationality and cultivates a greater intimacy with and responsibility for other creatures. Our answer to the question "Who is my neighbor?" can broaden to include concern for "brother sun and sister moon," in the words of St. Francis of Assisi.

It is not difficult to feel concern and act on it if the danger is in our back yard. Most of us will readily defend the health of the environment when it touches the perimeters of our own property and family. The difficulty arises when there is distance between us and the danger. The practice of solidarity raises our awareness and willingness to stand in defense of the larger world. It challenges our complacency with global affairs and stimulates our concern for creatures beyond our immediate neighborhood and nation.

What we do affects our survival and our health. It also affects others' ways of surviving and thriving. The practice of solidarity introduces a deeper sense of responsibility for checking the patterns by which we live to see how they impact that interdependency. From the vantage point of co-creators, we screen our behaviors for their life-giving capacity and their damaging repercussions. Respectfully and reverently, we acknowledge that what is done in one area of the planet affects the quality of life in another. This sixth discipline is a spiritual practice that becomes incarnated in deliberate actions and asceticism for the sake of the whole.

The Practice of Solidarity

How do we begin to practice solidarity as a spiritual discipline? We can shape our attempts by using a twofold approach: appropriate attitude and ascetical application. An appropriate, healthy attitude of solidarity that is flexible and compassionate needs to serve as the foundation for our ascetical application throughout our lives.

A Flexible, Appropriate Attitude of Compassion and Connectedness

We may be surprised to learn that, from a spiritual perspective, stridency against the inequities and injustices in the world may not be entirely helpful in developing an appropriate and healthy attitude. Justifiable anger can motivate us to act to change systems for the better. However, if our attitude becomes aggressive in our drive to effect change, this may give rise to a cynical and critical perspective which could lead to a breakdown in our healthy practice and concern. Pride, judgmentalism, and self-righteousness could emerge. These are never helpful in the spiritual life. Nor do they assist us in sustaining our enthusiasm to work for change, righting social injustices and indignities. We may develop a brittleness which can lead to fatigue and disappointment when changes are delayed. Burnout can result.

More helpful is a flexible attitude that engenders compassion and connectedness. Solidarity is about building a deliberate and felt sense of connectedness between ourselves, other human beings, and the environment. One way of fostering this is to continually refresh our awareness of our own vulnerability and that of others.

Our own compassion for others is often awakened by listening to their stories. In moments of openness and transparency, we may find ourselves resonating with others' struggles. Our hearts go out to them, and we are personally moved. We may discover that the differences that separate us have diminished and a new sense of appreciation and affinity has risen. Mercy mixes with respect and mutuality.

One of the greatest aids to our practice of solidarity is a refreshed sensitivity to our own and others' vulnerability. Condescension has no place here; mutuality takes precedence. In this context, permeated with compassion, a sense of solidarity can arise. It is in the tenderness of the heart rather than the critique of the mind that solidarity is sustained and deepened.

Eight Forms of Solidarity

Before we explore the ascetical application of solidarity, it may be helpful to identify some of the arenas in which solidarity may be experienced. What follows is a discussion of eight forms of solidarity.

1. Intimate-relational: As we mentioned in our discussion of the discipline of the sharing of stories, intimate-relational solidarity can emerge when persons are closely engaged, enjoying the resonance and support of one another. This form most readily occurs with loved ones with whom we trust our deepest selves. The core of who we are touches the core of them and a relationship that has longevity and nurturance can develop. Although friendships like this may be few in number, the feeling of being understood and personally accepted generates a solid sense of solidarity which can sustain us in times of trial and confusion.

2. Familial: Based on the sharing of a common heritage and bloodline, familial solidarity revolves around ancestry and historical relationship. This form of solidarity links us through blood and lineage to an assortment of relatives. While family relationships can be a source of many frustrations and irritations, a sense of familial solidarity can prevail over all of these, especially in times of suffering and loss. Funerals and illness can bring families together to grieve and support one another. Stories link the members through memory and obligation. The old adage "blood is thicker than water" is proved true. Celebrations like weddings and reunions also can unite a family and create new stories and associations that tie a family together. Blood ties have held kingdoms together in solidarity when war and dissension could have torn them apart. Familial solidarity is one form of solidarity that is often overlooked and even abused, but which deserves greater sensitivity and attentiveness in our practice.

3. Ecclesial: Our religious tradition binds us together with others in an extended community of faith. As in the case of the family, we find that our sense of solidarity as an ecclesial body grows even stronger when suffering, persecution, or loss occur. We share a common spiritual heritage which has been transmitted in an organized way throughout the centuries. This ties us together, despite differences in theology, language, and era. Watching the funeral of Cardinal Joseph Bernardin, members of the American Catholic Church grieved the loss of a leader whom they held dear. A felt sense of ecclesial solidarity united churchpersons together in belief, sorrow, and faith in God.

4. Ecumenical: The same funeral of Cardinal Bernardin also evoked a sense of ecumenical solidarity. In attendance at that funeral were leaders of numerous other religious bodies who gathered to bid farewell to someone they felt had upheld the common faith of Christianity and the dignity of humanity. Ecumenical solidarity incorporates a broader body of believers whose historical differences subside in moments such as these. Within Christianity, the love of Christ unifies persons with diverse approaches to the common faith. This form of solidarity has become more prevalent since the Second Vatican Council.

5. Political-Social: This may be the form of solidarity that is most familiar to many of us. Lech Walesa used the term "Solidarity" to name his movement for social and political change in Poland. Political-social solidarity involves active engagement with political and social structures to challenge unjust systems that undermine human dignity and freedom. Solidarity in this form brings together persons of many religions, lifestyles, nationalities, and orientations and unites them in pursuit of a common goal.

6. Liturgical: When we gather around a common table, worshiping at the altar of the Lord, we enter into a moment of solidarity that links us with the communion of saints from previous ages, all of whom gathered like this. We join in this liturgical celebration with others around the world who worship in the same way. The age-old experience of liturgy binds us symbolically, regardless of theological differences or prayer preferences. Our belief is that at this table we are one in the Body of Christ. Whether felt or simply believed, solidarity in communion is at the heart of this liturgical sacrament.

7. *Ministerial:* The shared work of ministry can bind us in solidarity. Whether we gather with other teachers at national conventions, form a pastoral team for the benefit of the parish, or reach out to our peers by serving as pastoral counselors, ministerial solidarity binds us to a common goal: service to the people of God. The ministry we do, whether salaried or volunteer, can tie us to others who are attempting to do the same. The sharing of our ideas, our frustrations, and our successes has the power to connect us with others who have similar concerns. When we come together, we share a mutual objective to minister effectively and contribute to the transformation of the world. Solidarity among ministers is crucial in an age when there are fewer and fewer clergy and people's needs are increasing. Ministers must bind together to collaborate in projects that maximize their competence and minimize their exhaustion.

8. *Mystical-Contemplative:* Thomas Merton, a Trappist monk, stood at the corner of 4th and Walnut in Louisville and experienced a profound sense of mystical-contemplative union with all of the strangers who passed by him.[2] Whether monk or activist, each of us can experience a sense of connectedness with persons throughout the world in prayer and meditation. We can resonate in the depths of our humanness with the whole of humanity and creation. Prepared by habitual prayer, we may experience this form of solidarity as a

graced moment of insight given by God. Divisions cease to be important and a deeper unity emerges. We break through our individual isolation and touch a foundational relationality that is pulsating, alive, and holy.

These are only eight of many forms of solidarity that we can experience. While some may not have been traditionally understood as forms of solidarity, all of them provide opportunities for experiencing and cultivating a greater sense of affinity. An expansion of our consciousness about each of them can help our practice.

We will not be able to simultaneously practice all eight of these forms to the same degree. Within the ebb and flow of life, different forms will take precedence at different times. At all times, however, we need to have an attitude that is flexible and compassionate and continually fosters an awareness of vulnerability and connectedness.

In my early twenties, I experienced a surge of enthusiasm for social justice. I joined groups that challenged unjust systems and institutions. I was single, healthy, and intellectually informed about the many ways in which I could fully live out my commitment to solidarity. In those days, the forms of solidarity which I practiced most were political-social, ecclesial, and mystical-contemplative.

In my thirties I went off to Africa to serve as a lay minister with a mission society. There I found my practice shifting to forms which included ecumenical, ministerial, and political-social solidarity "in the trenches" of active Third-World ministry.

After two years of overextension and increasingly disappointed idealism, I returned to the United States depleted emotionally and physically. I could no longer practice the political-social and ministerial solidarity to which

I had been devoting myself. Gradually, a quieter form of intimate-relational, familial, and liturgical solidarity began to evolve in my spirituality.

We must cultivate a flexibility that allows for adjustment in the forms of solidarity. The style of solidarity that we practiced in our youth will differ from that of our later years. There will be shifts in the way our zeal manifests itself. As we reformulate our practice of solidarity, we need to take into account family life, the realities of aging, life circumstances, and our own limitations. The emphasis in our practice of solidarity may change, but remaining open and eager to keep connected with a larger reality is essential in guiding our ascetical application.

The Ascetical Application of Solidarity

With an attitude of flexibility and compassion as our foundation, let us look more closely at the ascetical application of solidarity. We shape our lifestyles in response to the realization that we have a fundamental need for relationship to God and others. The asceticism of solidarity begins with reflecting on the various forms of solidarity and determining which of these forms are already in place in our lives. Second, in a reflective way through prayer and attentiveness, it involves identifying the areas where a stretching of our attitude and willingness to be concerned could occur.

God's invitations to us may appear in any of the eight arenas mentioned above. Ascetical applications will vary with the readiness and effort required emotionally, physically, and spiritually. Balance and readjustment in the forms will involve ongoing dialogue within ourselves, with sensitivity to our own limits and the needs of others. As we listen to the voice of God, we may find ourselves drawn beyond our self-imposed limits to a new level of selflessness and freedom.

God's invitation may surprise us. It may not be a stupendous summons, but rather a quiet call to move into an area of life where we would prefer not to go. Sometimes a long period of simpler responses readies us for a bigger task. Each application needs to be tested with gentleness and honesty.

Solidarity may mean being attentive to a friend who is in a serious struggle and needs extra care and patience. Stretching in familial solidarity may require reaching out in reconciliation to a relative from whom we are estranged. This may take as much or more ascetical effort as marching in a political-social protest against the pollution of a river or the proliferation of nuclear arms. We may feel the tug to more consciously address the plight of homeless persons through contributions to shelters or food banks. Our church or ecumenical community may need some of our skills to address these needs in an organized effort.

The important thing here is not to try to perform acts of solidarity in all of the arenas, but to be gently attentive to the tug of the Spirit as we are drawn into specific responses. Given the diversity of talents and the needs of the times and circumstances, each person's charism and call will be manifested differently.

The ascetical aspect of each response is often felt in the pruning that is entailed. Most likely, many of the responses of solidarity will involve a curbing of some of our strivings, compulsions, and preferences. We will need to apply some effort to evaluating the patterns of living to which we have become attached. Solidarity may require a change of schedule, a change of priorities, or a change of heart. It may even change our lives. Change is hard for most of us. The ascetical dimension of solidarity involves the type of change that stretches us beyond ourselves and our personal agendas. It opens us up to an interconnected universe, which is sustained by a sensitive give-and-take. That give-and-take may necessitate a tweaking of our proclivities to accumulate goods. The stretching involved in self-giving is a fundamental spiritual benefit of the practice of solidarity. We move beyond ourselves and our personal interests to respectfully respond to the larger needs of the human family and the planet.

Some of us will find that solidarity such as this broadens our horizons of concern. It may move us into service and political involvement, requiring profound personal prayer. It may take us into work that we had previously never imagined ourselves doing. This kind of stretching is absolutely necessary in an age when global realities affect everyone. The Spirit cultivates a readiness in the hearts of those needed to respond to the crises of the times. Persons who feel such a pull are advised to enter into discernment with skilled spiritual directors and pastoral counselors to determine how best to respond.

Whether our response takes place in the microcosm of our local community or in the macrocosm of a global project, it is important to anchor it in the bedrock of humility and attentiveness to God. Continual openness to the divine can help us maintain a healthy, grounded approach to service in the world. Inner nourishment by God through prayer, fellowship, and discernment is absolutely essential to a balanced expression of solidarity.

Living in the Tension: A Metaphor

A difficult reality in our practice of solidarity is the fact that we cannot "make it all better." We live in tension. No matter how hard we try, we will not be able to right all wrongs. Still, we must try. Our challenge is to live within the tension with grace and with concern for peoples of all hemispheres.

Living within the tension involves a certain faith that the contradictions inherent in human life are being reconciled in God, even when we logically cannot reconcile them ourselves. Here the interface between our practice of surrender and solidarity occurs. We live in the painful stretch between worlds, trying to live lives of simplicity, integrity, and service, while recognizing our limitations. Tension is inevitable. But, living gently with it is an ascetical discipline, too. Looking beyond our limited efforts and trusting in God is an act of surrender. The gracefulness of this letting-go and trusting God's providence is essential in keeping our practice of solidarity healthy, strong, and spiritually beneficial.

I recall as a young child going to the playground without any playmates. I learned quickly that I could still enjoy the teeter-totter if I shimmied up one side and carefully positioned myself in the middle over the fulcrum. I had to remain vigilant in balancing the two ends of the plank. As in skiing or standing on a moving bus, I had to stay firmly planted in my center but keep my legs bent flexibly so that I would not fall. If I locked my knees, I lost the flexibility and could not adjust to the shifts in weight.

Perhaps this can serve as a metaphor for the practice of solidarity. We stand at the fulcrum of many polarities in our world. They will pull at us, tug at our heart strings, and almost overwhelm us at times. We need to be flexibly attentive to the fluctuations underneath us, firmly grounded in balancing all the polarities which stand in tension with one another. With a gentle, relaxed, but attentive heart, we must find ways that are not rigid, condemnatory, or reactive. Without flexibility we could fall off the teeter-totter. We could become embittered by failure, lack of change, inevitable human foibles, the slow pace of change, or even failure. The result would be disillusionment followed by abandonment of the practice of solidarity altogether.

We must also be careful not to be seduced into a mindless, sleepy lifestyle that betrays the solidarity to which we have been challenged by the realities of our world and by our own spiritual insight. While the forms of solidarity we practice must be appropriate for the limits placed upon us at any given time, they must also reflect a clear, wise, respectful identification with those with whom we want to be connected.

Balancing on the teeter-totter, we must take a stance that is solid, focused, and flexible. When adversity threatens our effectiveness in one arena, we must be able to creatively shift our focus and entertain other possibilities. We must allow the current of compassion to flow through us to meet the needs of the world around us. Sometimes this will require a heroic act of self-transcendence that is recognized as such by others. At other times, it will require only a quiet, personal generosity of heart of which only God and we may be aware. All previous acts of solidarity, no matter how seemingly great or small, will prepare us for each succeeding act. Each act of kindness disposes us for the next. Solidarity is kindness and sensitive charity writ large.

When all of our efforts fall short, our practice of surrender must activate an attitude of trust. The full answering of needs is ultimately in bigger hands than our own. Surrender and solidarity remind us of that fundamental interdependence between ourselves, others, and God. We are part of a "bigger reality" and participate in something far greater than our human minds can comprehend. We are asked to contribute our part and surrender to that supreme mystery.

Questions for Our Practice of Solidarity

By slowing down, sharing our stories, giving ourselves to stillness and solitude, and surrendering to God, we are drawn into a deep form of solidarity at the heart of the world. Michael Crosby writes: "We discover ourselves there, in our heart, with God, but there we also discover ourselves in solidarity with the universe itself."[3] We become part of the very revelation of God when we bring this solidarity with humanity and creation into our solitude and then move out to act with reverence in ongoing service to the human community.

As we conclude this chapter on solidarity as a spiritual practice, a few questions may help us to assess our own practice and openness to the different forms of solidarity. Solidarity can be a difficult spiritual practice for us, because it demands both a stretching of our spiritual imagination to include persons and places we cannot see and a concrete application which may affect our lifestyle. A change in our practice of solidarity may require a systematic evaluation of our patterns of living.

The following questions can help us identify which forms of solidarity are already in place in our lives and where our practice of solidarity might grow.

In which arenas are you already aware of practicing some form of solidarity? Are some forms more comfortable for you?

*Where is God inviting you to stretch your atti-
tude of solidarity and willingness to be concerned?*

*Are there certain forms of solidarity that you re-
sist developing? What underlies the resistance?*

*What first step can you take to respond to God's
invitation?*

Epilogue

It was a wintry Sunday and I had just proclaimed
scripture as lector for the eucharistic liturgy, something I love to do. As the Mass continued, I was conscious of the fact that it had been a difficult week
and my heart was weighed down by many personal
and professional burdens. I felt alone, out of sorts,
and depressed.

From the lector's kneeler at the side of the altar, I
watched as our pastor lowered the host after the
Doxology, and I listened while he invited us to pray
the family prayer of our faith. I was closer to the altar
than usual and, as we raised our voices, I glanced up
at the stained-glass figures of the saints who surrounded this sacred space. Suddenly, I was aware of
countless others who had prayed this "Our Father"
throughout the centuries around an altar of faith.
My mentors of awareness, Teresa of Avila and John
of the Cross, Thomas Merton, Julian of Norwich,
and so many others had gathered around in trial and
testing and prayed this prayer. Their voices echoed
now in my own profession of trust and hope. I knew
their stories; they had fueled my flame for God. In
solidarity we spoke together this ancient invocation,
slowly, faithfully, in stillness and in solitude. We had

a shared faith and their examples now buoyed me up
and encouraged me to surrender to a God of mystery. I felt their presence, their support. On a contemplative level I knew that the communion of
saints embraced me and invited me to have courage.
I was part of a long historical lineage that honored
this eucharistic moment. I no longer felt so alone or
adrift.

We have come full circle around the wheel of the sixfold
path. The purpose of the six organic disciplines is to help us
cultivate a contemplative consciousness, one that allows us
to be touched by the mystery in the moment. These moments may be neither emotionally charged nor intense encounters that prompt a dramatic change. Rather, they may
be quiet, subtle experiences that uplift us and give us the
focus we need to live this particular day.

Traveling around the wheel of the sixfold path, we become more and more open to the mystery of God in everyday existence. It is interesting to note that, while the disciplines are not sequential, they are often experienced in the
same order in which they have been presented here. Slowing down, we become more available to the mystery in the
moment. Having entered into a contemplative rhythm, we
can share our stories more readily and receive others' sharing. As we step back into stillness after our sharing with
others, we absorb the breadth of that exchange and enter
into an interior solitude where we can quietly sift through
our reflections. Here we savor the insights that can bolster
our integrity, giving us the courage to stand firmly within
the truth of our persons in situations that might test our re-
solve to live truthful, honest lives. From those depths, a freedom to surrender our rigidities and unfreedoms emerges.

We let go of attachments and preoccupations that keep us away from others and God. We find new compassion surging and a greater connectedness from which we can act and care for others.

When our lifestyle accelerates and what is external begins to drive us, we must again consciously start proceeding around the wheel, slowing down on another level and moving progressively around the circle into deeper and deeper spirals of integration. The sixfold path is circled many times as we come into the center of who we are. We revisit each discipline as we can, as we are ready. We are stretched a little further with each visitation. Gradually, we move into the depths of our core and know that each of the six practices has enriched us. All of these practices lead to the center.

The six spiritual practices in this book are identified as organic because they spring from the fundamental rhythms of daily life. There is nothing extraordinary about them or our practice of them. There may be certain disciplines to which we find ourselves naturally attracted. They are easier for us. We naturally gravitate toward a practice of these and find ourselves inclined toward them because of our temperament or experience.

There are other practices that we find ourselves resisting. They are more difficult for us to build into our lives and we find ourselves tending to shy away from them. We may even feel a slight revulsion to these practices and would prefer not to be challenged in our application of them. Stretching in the spiritual life involves reflecting on our areas of resistance and addressing the underlying obstacles that prevent us from moving into deeper levels of integration.

The sixfold path outlined in this book is simple. We do not have to be spiritual athletes to exercise the mindfulness that has been outlined here. But we do need to be deliberate. We also need to strategize a bit in order to plan how we can incorporate each of the spiritual disciplines into our lives.

This is an epilogue, my last words so far on this topic. I think it would be remiss of me as an author to end this book without mentioning some of the practical ways in which these disciplines can be fostered in the concreteness of daily life. Some of the suggestions that follow come from my own experience; the rest come from insights shared by other practitioners. These final ten suggestions could be viewed as tips for the integration of the organic spiritual disciplines. The suggestions are simple and practical, but they can be powerful aids in fostering spiritual growth.

Suggestions for Sixfold Success

1. Learn to breathe. At certain points in our day, many of us find ourselves holding our breath. This is not conducive to fullness of life. Breathing is a primary rhythm for physical survival, but it also has important spiritual ramifications. The depth of our breathing is an indicator, not just of our physical condition, but also of our spiritual state. A spiritual teacher I know used to invite his disciples to breathe each breath "as if it were your last." In other words, be deliberate, mindful, and thorough. Check the level of your breathing several times during the day. Intentionally stop and focus on breathing more deeply. Feel it. Note the difference. When you find yourself tensing up, breathe more deeply. Periodically relax the muscles of your diaphragm. Consciously breathe into them. This will enable you to more easily slow down, be still, enter into solitude, and let go.

2. Pad your schedule. I learned from sprinting down the hall between appointments that breathing and focusing take time. So does orienting ourselves in order to clear the way for the next event on the agenda. I learned that no one was going to take care of that for me. Nor could I depend on anyone else to provide me with breaks so that I could reconnect internally. Padding our schedules can give us just a little edge on sanity in the middle of insane days...a breather, if nothing else. It can be the space needed to remind us that slowing down is valuable, stillness is needed, and solitude is possible even in the midst of very busy schedules. Leaving a cushion of time between appointments allows us to regroup, adjust, and ground ourselves before moving too quickly into the next encounter. Another way to pad our schedule is to limit the undertakings and plans for a given period of time to *one* item, one meeting, one task, or one event. This is difficult with active children, I know. Some parents find that limiting extracurricular involvements to one sport per season helps. It is especially important to reclaim the evening and allow it to become a time that is less congested, slower, and more reflective. This will help with better sleep and living more gracefully.

3. Use delays for spiritual enrichment. Turnpikes can really irritate me, especially when traffic is backed up. But I have begun to utilize traffic delays for spiritual enrichment. Sometimes that means consciously praying for some of the drivers surrounding me. Sometimes it means breathing more intentionally and stretching my tensed neck and shoulder muscles. Sometimes it is a time to connect verbally with God through reflection or in silence. Inspirational music can help soothe the irritation. There are even good spiritual books on tape that can accompany a long journey. If your next appointment is delayed, breathe, close your eyes, and stretch out. This could be a divine moment.

4. Post reminders for your ongoing formation. I mentioned earlier that I have a high metabolism that inclines me toward rushing. To practice slowing down, I must employ tools that reinforce my decision to revise my tendency to rush. Some of the means that I have devised to assist myself include visual catalysts and internal and external verbal reminders. As a visual catalyst, I have chosen to decorate my office in colors and images that foster a more contemplative pace for my guests, as well as for myself. Verbal help may come from internal mantras that include words like, "focus," "take your time," or "breathe." For years I have also cut out or copied short quotes from various sources of wisdom that reinforce my decision to move more slowly. These are taped above my computer, as a reminder while I work, and on the back of my door, so they are the last thing I see before I bolt into the world. They are also taped near my mirror so that I can remind myself each time I check my appearance. These reminders serve as invitations to physically take a slow, deep breath and begin again my practice in a more conscious and deliberate frame of mind.

5. Note the position of your hands and the feeling of your muscles during the day. When we get tense, we often curl up our hands. We form fists to steel us for the stress. Our clenched fingers silently express our need to grab at control. The muscles in our stomachs, our jaws, our necks, and our spines also tense up. Most of us know the places where we store tension in our bodies. Periodically in the day, focus on those places. Check the degree of tension in them. Try letting go into a loose, more open posture. When you are sitting at meetings or on the bus, note if your hands are open and receptive in a contemplatively relaxed way. Stretch them and reinforce your awareness of remaining open to God. Let them become indicators of your fundamental attitude of surrender to God in the world.

6. Review your day for awe and wonder. Take some time to review the day for moments of awe and wonder. Note how you received them. If you missed them, or dismissed them, how could you cultivate greater receptivity the next time? Do this at least once or twice a day (noon and evening). It can help heighten awareness, opening our eyes to little things that begin to present themselves for greater appreciation. In another form, Saint Ignatius of Loyola suggests an examen of conscience through which we can assess frequently each day where we are in sync with the rhythm and invitation of the Spirit and where we may have deviated. Checking in with God before lunch and before dinner in a brief review of our attentiveness of heart over the past few hours can raise our awareness of God's presence and of alternative ways to respond to the challenges ahead.

7. Focus on the small and the simple. Slow down inside in order to relish the tiny gifts of the day. Let your consciousness notice the small wonders that, like cactus flowers in the desert, subtle and almost unnoticeable, can uplift you, bring delight, and spread goodness. Each day, choose to do one thing with total attentiveness, whether it is drinking a cup of coffee, touching someone you love, or massaging lotion into your skin. Extend your consciousness of charity. Try to perform three acts of charity *before* you arrive at work each morning. Most likely, this practice will change your driving or walking attitude and direct that day's consciousness toward the basics of gentility, civility, and courtesy. Recover virtue and little acts of charity in your everyday life.

8. Write. Record your experiences, your stories, your memories. Write letters, but instead of mailing them, save them for a journal box. Reread them at the end of the month. Write down the next set of images and thoughts that come. This will open up your reflective capacities and prepare you to share your story and make connections.

9. Laugh. A lot. Zen tells us that laughter for a few minutes in the morning is as good as several hours of sitting meditation. Laughter loosens up all the breathing muscles and abdominal organs, so that a greater sense of relaxation and ease can flow through us physically and emotionally. We become less constricted and "uptight." Laughter also reminds us that we should not take ourselves too seriously. Surrender flows very readily from an amused and detached heart.

10. Review your practice of the six disciplines. Every six months, take a morning or afternoon to reflectively assess your approach to the sixfold path. See which disciplines organically are most apparent in your life at that point. Identify the ones that are less apparent. Let the questions at the end of each chapter guide your reflection. If it is too difficult to reflect on all six disciplines, select a different one each month and spread out your reflection. Record your observations so that you can return to them in the future. As you review your practice, reflect honestly on where the Spirit may be inviting you to go in the next stage of your spiritual life. Prayerfully allow yourself to take in the invitation and become aware of your response. Be gentle and firm with yourself in this appraisal. Let it be a spiritual encounter with God that guides your self-awareness and growth.

All of these suggestions for sixfold success are offered for one purpose only: to deepen intimacy with God. That is the main passion of the spiritual life. Whatever organic, religious, or vocational influences assist us in moving more readily into intimacy with the divine, we have one lifetime to take them up and act upon them. Our bodies will clue us in to what affects our hearts and is right for us.

Follow the fire that burns within you. Like the Israelites pursuing the column of fire by night, trust that the Mystery of God will lead you from slavery through the desert of hungers to fill the deepest desires of your heart. Stay with the journey. Remain actively engaged in it. And God will meet you every step of the way.

Notes

A Definition of Spirituality

1. I am grateful to Vincent Bilotta, Ph.D., of Formation Consultation Services, Inc. for numerous conversations (1993–1995) which helped clarify this definition.

2. *Webster's New Collegiate Dictionary* (Springfield, Mass.: G. & C. Merriam, 1977), 605.

Organic Spirituality: What Is It?

1. *Webster's New Collegiate Dictionary* (Springfield, Mass.: G. & C. Merriam, 1977), 808.

2. Adrian van Kaam identifies four dimensions of the human person in his anthropology. He names sociohistoric, vital, functional, and transcendent dimensions as important in human formation, and notes that the last of these, the transcendent dimension, distinguishes the human person as a spiritual being. See Adrian van Kaam, *Formative Spirituality: Fundamental Formation*, vol. 1 (New York, N.Y.: Crossroad, 1983).

An Introduction to the Sixfold Path

1. Adrian van Kaam, *Spirituality and the Gentle Life* (Pittsburgh, Pa.: Epiphany Books, 1994), 9.

2. Buddhist philosophy invites the devotee to practice the eight disciplines of right vision, right effort, right speech, right intention, right concentration, right mindfulness, right action, and right livelihood. Often these practices are depicted as a wheel with eight spokes, all leading to the center. The practice of one reinforces and aids the development of the others in leading the devotee to a deeper spiritual level.

3. See Ronald Rolheiser, OMI, *Shattered Lanterns* (New York, N.Y.: Crossroad, 1995), specifically chapter 3, "Narcissism, Pragmatism, and Unbridled Restlessness," 24ff.

4. Adrian van Kaam coins this term in reference to ministers and clergy who think they should always be on call, with few personal boundaries or inviolable private time.

Slowing Down

1. Numerous techniques which extend from meditation to forms of stress reduction are available to assist in the slowing down process. Two books that deal with slowing down on a physical level are Herbert Benson, *The Relaxation Response* (New York, N.Y.: Avon Books, 1975) and Alexander and Leslie Lowen, *The Way to Vibrant Health: A Manual of Bioenergetic Exercises* (New York, N.Y.: Harper Colophon Books, 1977). Books on techniques that involve meditation include Anthony de Mello, *Sadhana: A Way to God* (Garden City, N.Y.: Image Books, 1984) and Thich Nhat Hanh, *Peace Is Every Step: The Path of Mindfulness in Everyday Life* (New York: Bantam Books, 1992).

2. Appraisal is conventionally understood in Christianity as discretion or discernment in which we "discover, evaluate and decide to act or refrain from acting in tune with [our] presence to particular aspects of [our] life." See Carolyn Gratton, *The Art of Spiritual Guidance* (New York, N.Y.: Crossroad, 1992), 171.

3. Belden C. Lane, "Desert Attentiveness, Desert Indifference: Countercultural Spirituality in the Desert Fathers and Mothers," *Crosscurrents* (Summer 1994), 197.

Sharing Our Stories

1. See Dorotheus of Gaza, *Discourses and Sayings*, trans. Eric P. Wheeler, Cistercian Studies Series, No. 33 (Kalamazoo, Mich.: Cistercian Publications, 1977), 122.

Stillness

1. See Brother David Steindl-Rast, *Gratefulness, the Heart of Prayer: An Approach to Life in Fullness* (Ramsey, N.J.: Paulist Press, 1984), 71.

2. Sue Monk Kidd, *When the Heart Waits: Spiritual Direction for Life's Sacred Questions* (San Francisco, Calif.: Harper and Row, 1990), 127.

Solitude

1. Thomas Merton, *Thoughts in Solitude* (New York, N.Y.: Image Books, 1958), 13.

2. Carolyn Gratton, *The Art of Spiritual Guidance* (New York, N.Y.: Crossroad, 1992), 120.

3. Merton, *Thoughts in Solitude*, 79.

4. Sue Monk Kidd, *When the Heart Waits: Spiritual Direction for Life's Sacred Questions* (San Francisco, Calif.: Harper and Row, 1990), 127.

5. Thomas Merton, *New Seeds of Contemplation* (New York, N.Y.: New Directions, 1972), 80.

Surrender

1. Thomas Merton, *Thoughts in Solitude* (New York, N.Y.: Image Books, 1958), 20.

2. Ibid., 31.

3. Julian of Norwich, *Showings*, trans. Edmund Colledge, O.S.A. and James Walsh, S. J. (New York, N.Y.: Paulist Press, 1978), 305.

4. Thomas Merton speaks of these attachments in *New Seeds of Contemplation* (New York, N.Y.: New Directions, 1961), 257-58. John of the Cross also instructs us on these attachments in his classic work on the spiritual journey, *The Ascent of Mount Carmel*. See *The Collected Works of St. John of the Cross*, trans. Kieran Kavanaugh, O.C.D., and Otilio Rodriguez, O.C.D. (Washington, D.C.: ICS Publications, 1979).

5. See St. Ignatius of Loyola, *The Spiritual Exercises of St. Ignatius: A Literal and a Contemporary Reading*, trans. David L. Fleming, S.J. (St. Louis, Mo.: The Institute of Jesuit Sources, 1978).

Solidarity

1. Adrian van Kaam, *Formation of the Human Heart*, vol. 3. Formative Spirituality Series (New York, N.Y.: Crossroad, 1986), 223.

2. See Thomas Merton, *Conjectures of a Guilty Bystander* (Garden City, N.Y.: Doubleday Image Books, 1989), 156-58.

3. Michael Crosby, *Spirituality of the Beatitudes: Matthew's Challenge for First World Christians* (Maryknoll, N.Y.: Orbis, 1981), 173.

Bibliography

Benson, Herbert. *The Relaxation Response*. New York, N.Y.: Avon Books, 1975.

Crosby, Michael. *Spirituality of the Beatitudes: Matthew's Challenge for First World Christians*. Maryknoll, N.Y.: Orbis, 1981.

de Mello, Anthony. *Sadhana: A Way to God*. Garden City, N.Y.: Image Books, 1984.

Dorotheus of Gaza. *Discourses and Sayings*. Trans. Eric P. Wheeler, Cistercian Studies Series, No. 33, Kalamazoo, Mich.: Cistercian Publications, 1977.

Gratton, Carolyn. *The Art of Spiritual Guidance*. New York: Crossroad, 1992.

Ignatius of Loyola. *The Spiritual Exercises of St. Ignatius: A Literal and a Contemporary Reading*. Trans. David L. Fleming, S.J. St. Louis, Mo.: The Institute of Jesuit Sources, 1978.

John of the Cross. *The Collected Works of St. John of the Cross*. Trans. Kieran Kavanaugh, O.C.D., and Otilio Rodriguez, O.C.D. Washington, D.C.: ICS Publications, 1979.

Julian of Norwich. *Showings*. Trans. Edmund Colledge, O.S.A., and James Walsh, S. J. New York, N.Y.: Paulist Press, 1978.

Lane, Belden C. "Desert Attentiveness, Desert Indifference: Countercultural Spirituality in the Desert Fathers and Mothers," *Crosscurrents* (Summer 1994), 197.

Lowen, Alexander and Leslie. *The Way to Vibrant Health: A Manual of Bioenergetic Exercises*. New York, N.Y.: Harper Colophon Books, 1977.

Merton, Thomas. *Conjectures of a Guilty Bystander*. Garden City, N.Y.: Doubleday Image Books, 1989.

————. *New Seeds of Contemplation.* New York, N.Y.: New Directions, 1961, 1972.

————. *Thoughts in Solitude.* New York, N.Y.: Image Books, 1958.

Monk Kidd, Sue. *When the Heart Waits: Spiritual Direction for Life's Sacred Questions.* San Francisco, Calif.: Harper and Row, 1990.

Nhat Hanh, Thich. *Peace Is Every Step: The Path of Mindfulness in Everyday Life.* New York, N.Y.: Bantam Books, 1992.

Rolheiser, Ronald, OMI. *Shattered Lanterns.* New York, N.Y.: Crossroad, 1995.

Steindl-Rast, Brother David. *Gratefulness, the Heart of Prayer: An Approach to Life in Fullness.* Ramsey, N.J.: Paulist Press, 1984.

van Kaam, Adrian. *Formation of the Human Heart.* Formative Spirituality Series, Vol. 3. New York, N.Y.: Crossroad, 1986.

————. *Fundamental Formation.* Formative Spirituality Series, Vol. 1. New York, N.Y.: Crossroad, 1983.

————. *In Search of Spiritual Identity.* Denville, N.J.: Dimension Books, 1975.

————. *Spirituality and the Gentle Life.* Pittsburgh, Pa.: Epiphany Books, 1994.

Webster's New Collegiate Dictionary. Springfield, Mass.: G. & C. Merriam, 1977.